101 Keto Diet Slow Cooker Recipes

Easy, Delicious, and Healthy Low-Carb Crock Pot Recipes

By

Kristina Newman

As a "Thank You" for purchasing this book, I want to give you a gift absolutely 100% Free

** Follow the instructions at the end of this book to receive Keto Holiday Recipes FREE **

Table of Contents

Introduction

Congratulations and Thank You!

I want to start by thanking you for downloading the book, "*Ketogenic Diet Dinner Recipes: 125 Quick, Easy Low Carb, Keto Meals*" I am honored to be helping you on this journey to create easy, healthy Keto recipes!

These days, there are a variety of diet regimens that promise full-body health; not only will you lose weight in your problem areas, you will also experience a total health transformation with your digestive system, your metabolism, and other components. The ketogenic diet is one of the better dietary options if you are looking for this total-body experience and beginning on your path toward looking great and speeding up your metabolism for a healthier lifestyle. The great part about the Keto diet, as it is known, is that it is so compatible with different tastes and modes of preparation. Slow cookers, for example, are a great tool to utilize if you are looking for ways to prepare your keto-friendly meals. Seeing as the ketogenic diet relies heavily on protein rich foods such as meats and vegetables, a slow cooker is the perfect way to make wholesome, delicious meals that keep you on track with the regimen.

However, if you find yourself at a loss as to how to stay on track with your meals, look no further than the following pages of this e-book. You will find 101 Keto recipes that are simple, tasty, and can be prepared in a slow cooker, which is a great way to create satisfying meals with relatively low involvement. The 'set it and forget it' method of using a slow cooker is convenient for you, and also brings out the rich flavors of the food you are cooking. This e-book will therefore show you how easy it is to combine the lifestyle changes of the ketogenic diet with the convenience of slow cooking, and never will you feel that you have sacrificed the taste of your food!

Thanks again for downloading this book, I Hope You Enjoy It

What is the Ketogenic Diet? (Keto Diet)

Despite the many different kinds of diets that you have no doubt heard about in your life, there is bound to be a few that are new to you. One of these in particular might be the Ketogenic Diet, also known as the Keto Diet, which is a high-fat, low-carbohydrate regimen. The theory behind the high-fat, low-carbohydrate ratio is that the body will rely on fat for energy instead of on carbohydrates, and therefore the body will become more lean as a result of having less fat stored in the body. Ideally, the Keto Diet will allow the body to go into ketosis, or a metabolic state where ketones - which are fats - are burned for energy instead of glucose - the carbohydrates. Those that follow the Keto Diet also consume just the right amount of protein that the body needs on a daily basis. Contrary to some of the other diets that are in existence, the Keto Diet does not focus on counting calories. The focus is instead centered on the fat, carbohydrate, and protein make-up of the food as well as on the weight of the portions.

But what led to the creation of the Keto Diet? Back in 1924, a Mayo Clinic doctor by the name of Russell Wilder developed the Ketogenic Diet in hopes of finding a treatment for epilepsy. Many people who suffer from epilepsy and other illnesses have reported a noticeable decrease in their symptoms after going on this diet. This practice dates back to Ancient Greece when doctors would change their patients' diets and even have them fast to force their body into starvation mode. The Ketogenic Diet is a much easier means of getting the body to go into the fasting mode without actually depriving the body of food. To this day, however, no one knows exactly why the Ketogenic Diet is so effective in helping those that suffer from epilepsy, autism, and other known illnesses.

A typical meal for someone on the Ketogenic Diet would feature the high-fat, low-carbohydrate ratio, and might include a healthy serving of a protein such as chicken, some fruit or a protein-rich vegetable, and a high-fat component, which might be butter. The high-fat component on this diet usually comes from the ingredients which go into making the food; this could include heavy cream, butter, or buttermilk, and also might feature creamy dressings such as Ranch.

Why Choose the Ketogenic Diet?

Over the years, researchers have found that there are many benefits to choosing the Ketogenic Diet. There was initial speculation that the diet would cause a cholesterol build-up in the body, therefore leading to heart disease due to the high-fat content of the foods that people on the diet could consume. However, as more and more experts have looked into the diet, they have found that there are inherent advantages for beginning this type of diet. For one, the body is able to utilize fat instead of carbohydrates for energy. The body will therefore not rely on carbohydrates since there is such a low amount entering the body, and will thus be able to store ketones - the fats - for later energy use.

Another benefit is the fact that the body will not be as hungry, and people on the Keto Diet therefore are at a lower risk of falling off their regiment by snacking. Because the Keto Diet encourages the consumption of various protein-rich foods which work to curb hunger. The body goes into the state of ketosis - which is common among those who fast regularly - and therefore does not require a lot of food to keep it going. What better than to be on a healthy diet and not have constant hunger pangs?

Finally, the health benefits offered by the Keto Diet are remarkable. People who follow the Keto Diet completely eliminate starchy carbohydrates, such as breads and pastas, and substitute them with non-starch vegetables such as broccoli, asparagus, carrots, and many others. These kinds of vegetables are packed with vitamins and nutrients that support a healthy body, and are also much lower in calories. The Keto Diet, in addition to aiding those who suffer from illnesses such as epilepsy, is also recommended for cancer patients. As research has shown, cancer cells flourish in areas of the body where there is a lot of glucose, which is what carbohydrates become. If the body consumes less carbohydrates, there will therefore be less glucose, and subsequently the cancer cells will not be able to grow and thrive.

Benefits Of A Keto Diet

•Cholesterol. A Keto diet has shown to improve triglyceride levels and cholesterol levels most associated with arterial buildup.

•Weight Loss. As your body is burning fat as the main source of energy, you will essentially be using your fat stores as an energy source while in a fasting state.

•Blood Sugar. Many studies show the decrease of LDL cholesterol over time and have shown to eliminate ailments such as type 2 diabetes.

•Energy. By giving your body a better and more reliable energy source, you will feel more energized during the day. Fats are shown to be the most effective molecule to burn as fuel.

•Hunger. Fat is naturally more satisfying and ends up leaving us in a satiated ("full") state for longer.

•Acne. Recent studies have shown a drop in acne lesions and skin inflammation over 12 weeks.

Slow Cooker Tips and Tricks

Get helpful tips for turning your slow cooker recipe into an even better slow-cooked meal.

The beauty of using a slow cooker or crock pot is that it's pretty darn simple. Prep your ingredients, add them to the slow cooker and press Start. But there is a difference between a good slow-cooker meal and a great slow-cooker meal. Here are some tips to keep in mind when you're using your slow cooker or crock pot

Head Start

If you're short on time in the morning, prepare everything you need for your slow-cooked meal the night before, put it into the slow-cooker dish, cover and store in the fridge overnight. Ideally the dish should be as close to room temperature as possible, so get it out of the fridge when you wake up and leave it for 20 minutes before turning the cooker on. If you need to heat your dish beforehand, then put the ingredients in a different container and transfer them in the morning.

Trim the fat

You don't need to add oil to a slow cooker, the contents won't catch as long as there's enough moisture in there. You don't need a lot of fat on your meat either. Normally when you fry meat, a lot of the fat drains away, this won't happen in a slow cooker so trim it off, otherwise you might find you have pools of oil in your stew. This will give you a healthier result and it'll still be tasty.

Don't use frozen food:

Loading a slow cooker with icy ingredients will keep food in the danger zone where bacteria can flourish (40 to 140 degrees F). So make sure your meat and vegetables are fully thawed before turning the cooker on. The exception: Prepackaged slow-cooker meals sold in the freezer case are fine to use as long as you follow the package's directions.

Light on the liquid

Because your slow cooker will have a tightly sealed lid, the liquid won't evaporate so if you're adapting a standard recipe, it's best to reduce the liquid by roughly a third. Liquid should just cover the meat and vegetables. Don't overfill your slow cooker or it may start leaking out the top and food won't cook as well. Half to two thirds full is ideal and certainly no more than three quarters.

Thickening

Just as the liquid doesn't reduce it also doesn't thicken. You can roll meat in a small amount of seasoned flour before adding it to the slow cooker or use a little corn flour at the end. If you want to do the latter, take a teaspoon or two of corn flour, mix it to a paste with a little cold water. Stir into your simmering slow cooker contents, and then replace the lid.

Avoid Over Filling

For the best results, fill a slow cooker between one-half and two-thirds full. Go ahead and cook big roasts and whole chickens; just make sure you use a large crock and that the lid fits snugly on top.

Slow is good

Use the 'Low' setting as much as you can, most dishes really benefit from a slow, gentle heat to really bring out the flavors.

Add Dairy Last

Sour cream, milk and yogurt tend to break down in the slow cooker, so stir them in during the last 15 minutes of cooking.

Leave it alone

Slow cookers are designed to do their own thing so you don't need to keep checking the contents. Every time you take the lid off it will release some of the heat, so if you keep doing this you'll have to increase the cooking time.

101 Keto Slow Cooker Recipes

Here you will find fun and easy Keto Recipes Have Fun!!

Spicy Chicken Enchilada Soup

INGREDIENTS:

1 1/2 lbs. boneless skinless chicken breasts
1 medium yellow onion, diced
1 bell pepper, thinly sliced
1 jalapeno, diced
2 cloves garlic, minced
1 15-oz. can diced tomatoes
2 cups chicken stock
1 tbsp chili powder
1 tbsp cumin
1 tsp dried oregano
1/2 tsp paprika
Salt and freshly ground pepper, to taste
2 tbsp fresh cilantro, chopped
1 avocado, pitted and sliced

INSTRUCTIONS:

•Insert the chicken breasts into the bottom of a crockpot.
•Place the diced onion, sliced pepper and jalapeno and the minced garlic on top of the meat.
•Add the diced tomatoes and the 2 cups of chicken stock into the crockpot.
•Sprinkle the spices and adjust seasonings with salt and pepper.
•Place lid, cover and allow the ingredients to cook for about 8 hours on low.
•Once the chicken is tender shred the meat using a fork.
•Serve with avocado and cilantro.

Crockpot Cabbage and Corned Beef Delight

INGREDIENTS:

1 Small Onion
1 Celery bunch
4 Carrots
4 Cups Water
½ tsp Ground Coriander
½ tsp Ground Mustard
½ tsp Black Pepper
½ tsp Salt
½ tsp Allspice
½ tsp Ground Marjoram
½ tsp Ground Thyme
5.88 lb Corned Beef
1 Large Head Cabbage (1.33 kg)

INSTRUCTIONS:

•Slice the small onion, carrots and celery into fine pieces.
•Lay the sliced vegetables inside the crockpot.
•Pour about 4 cups of water over the ingredients.
•Place all the spices in a bowl and mix well.
•Toss in the corned beef into the bowl and marinade well.
•Leave the seasoned beef on top of the vegetables in the crockpot.
•Place lid, cover and cook for about 7 hours on a low heat.
•Remove the first layer of the large cabbage, rinse with water and cut into 4 pieces.
•Toss in the cabbage pieces into the crockpot.
•Mix well and leave for about another hour on low.
•Serve warm and enjoy!

Beef Stroganoff and Mushroom Soup

INGREDIENTS:

32 oz. Beef Stock
10 oz. Cremini Mushrooms – Thinly Sliced
1 Medium Onion – Diced
3 Tbs. Garlic – Minced
3 Tbs. Butter
1 ½ lbs. Steak – Thinly Sliced
1 Cup Heavy Cream
1 Cup Sour Cream
2 Tbs. Beef Bouillon Granules
2 Tbs. Dijon Mustard
2. Tbs. Italian Flat Leaf Parsley – Chopped
1 ½ tsp. Onion Powder
1 ½ tsp. Garlic Powder
1 tsp. Dried Oregano
1 tsp. Sea Salt
(2 Tbs. Peace and Love)

INSTRUCTIONS:

•Place the sliced mushrooms into the crockpot.
•Pour the beef stock over the mushrooms and cover the cooker with the lid.
•Heat a skillet on a medium heat and melt the butter.
•Toss in the diced onions and garlic and leave until the ingredients are soft.
•Add the sautéed ingredients into the crockpot.
•Heat the steak using the same skillet and brown on both sides for about 2 minutes.
•Place the browned steak into the crockpot over the onions and garlic.
•Pour the sour cream and heavy cream over the ingredients.
•Add the beef bouillon granules, parsley, mustard, onion and garlic powder, oregano and salt.
•Leave for 6 hours on high until the ingredients are cooked and tender.

Creamy Chicken and Noodles

INGREDIENTS:

2 pounds chicken breast tenders
1 large onion, chopped
1 large pepper, chopped
1 teaspoon salt
½ teaspoon oregano
½ teaspoon garlic powder
½ teaspoon thyme
¼ teaspoon pepper
1 cup sour cream
1 cup shredded cheddar cheese
4 medium zucchini, julienned into noodles

INSTRUCTIONS:

•Season the chicken breast tenders with salt and pepper.
•Place the chicken in the crockpot and add the onion, garlic powder, thyme, oregano and chopped pepper.
•Place lid, cover and allow to cook for about 6-8 hours on low.
•Transfer the chicken into a platter and shred the meat.
•Place the shredded meat once again into the crockpot.
•Toss in the zucchini, cheese and then the sour cream.
•Leave for about 30 minutes until the zucchini becomes soft and tender.
•Serve using a slotted spoon.

Keto Pulled Pork

INGREDIENTS:

2 lbs of pork shoulder (or tenderloin)
1 can of diet pop (root beer or Dr. Pepper)
a dash of cinnamon
chipotle sauce
hot sauce
4 oz of low carb/sugar free bbq sauce

INSTRUCTIONS:

•Place the pork shoulder in a crockpot.
•Sprinkle a dash of cinnamon and pour the diet pop into the crockpot.
•Allow the meat to cook for about 6-7 hours on low.
•Remove the ingredients after the cooking time.
•Serve the tender meat with the sauces as required.

Mushroom and Chicken Bacon Chowder

INGREDIENTS:

4 Cloves Garlic – Minced
1 Shallot – Finely Chopped
1 Leek – Cleaned, Trimmed, and Sliced
2 Ribs Celery – Diced
6 oz. Cremini Mushrooms – Sliced
1 Medium Sweet Onion – Thinly Sliced
4 Tbs. Butter – Divided
2 Cups Chicken Stock – Divided
1 lb. Boneless, Skinless Chicken Breasts
8 oz. Cream Cheese
1 Cup Heavy Cream
1 lb. Bacon – Cooked Crisp, and Crumbled
1 tsp. Salt
1 tsp. Pepper
1 tsp. Garlic Powder
1 tsp. Thyme
(2 Tbs. Peace and Love)

INSTRUCTIONS:

•Place the shallot, garlic, leek, mushrooms, celery, onions, butter (2 tbsps), salt and pepper into the crockpot.
•Pour about 1 cup of stock over the ingredients and mix well.
•Place lid and cook the ingredients for 1 hour on low.
•In the meantime, heat a skillet and melt the balance 2 tbsps of butter.
•Place the chicken and brown on both sides for 5 minutes per side.
•Transfer the browned chicken into a plate.
•Pour the balance stock into the skillet and remove any chicken shreds left in the pan.
•Add the stock into the crockpot along with the heavy cream, garlic powder, cream cheese and thyme.
•Continue to stir until the cream cheese is completely dissolved and no pieces seen in the mixture.
•Shred the chicken and place in the crockpot.
•Mix in the bacon and combine all ingredients together.
•Place lid, cover and let the ingredients cook for about 6-8 hours on low.

Spicy Beef in Crockpot – Low Carb and Gluten Free

INGREDIENTS:

2.5 lb Chuck Roast
6 Tbsp Coconut Milk Powder (see note at bottom of post)
2 cups water
3 Tbsp Red Curry Paste
5 cardamom pods, cracked
2 Tbsp Thai fish sauce
1 Tbsp dried onion flakes
2 Tbsp dried thai chilis (or fresh red chilis)
1 Tbsp granulated sugar substitute
1 Tbsp ground cumin
1 Tbsp ground coriander
1/8 tsp ground cloves
1/8 tsp ground nutmeg
1 Tbsp ground ginger
To Serve:
2 Tbsp coconut milk powder
1 Tbsp red curry paste
2 Tbsp granulated sugar substitute
1/4 tsp xanthan gum (optional)
1/4 cup cashews, roughly chopped
1/4 cup fresh cilantro, chopped

INSTRUCTIONS:

•Insert the chuck roast into a crockpot.
•Mix in about 6 tbsp coconut milk, 3 tbsp curry paste, cardamom pods, fish sauce onion flakes, 1 tbsp sweetener, chilis, coriander, cumin, nutmeg, cloves and ginger.
•Pour the water over the ingredients and mix well.
•Place lid, cover and allow the ingredients to cook for about 5 hours on high or for 8 hours on low.
•Transfer the meat into a platter once cooked.
•Mix the sauce with 2 tbsp coconut milk powder, 2 tbsp sweetener, 1 tbsp curry paste and ¼ tsp gum (optional).
•Shred the meat and dip into the sauce.
•Add the chopped cashew nuts into the sauce and serve garnished with cilantro.
•Ideal to be served with cauliflower rice.

Jerk Chicken in Crockpot

INGREDIENTS:

8 scallions, chopped coarse
1/4 cup vegetable oil
2 habanero chilies, stemmed and seeded
1 (1-inch) fresh ginger, peeled and sliced 1/4 inch thick
2 tablespoons molasses
3 garlic cloves, peeled
1 tablespoon thyme
2 teaspoons allspice
1/4 teaspoon cardamom
1 teaspoon coarse salt
4 pounds bone-in, skin-on chicken pieces (split breasts, thighs)
lime wedges for serving

INSTRUCTIONS:

•Insert the scallion, habaneros, molasses, ginger, garlic, all spice, thyme, cardamom and salt into a food processor.
•Add the oil and process well.
•Remove about ½ cup of the mixture into a slow cooker and leave the balance aside.
•Insert the chicken into the crockpot and rub well with the scallion mix.
•Place lid, cover and allow to cook on low for 4-6 hours.
•Rack should be positioned about 10" from the broiler element and then start the broiler.
•Lightly spray a rack covered with foil with a vegetable spray and place the chicken with the skin side facing the rack.
•Rub the meat with the kept aside scallion mix and broil for about 12-15 minutes until crisp.
•Turn the chicken onto the other side and season with the balance scallion mix.
•Leave the chicken to broil for about another 8-10 minutes to brown on the other side.
•Serve garnished with lime wedges.
•Enjoy!

Crockpot Pork and Bacon Carnitas

INGREDIENTS:

8 Lb Boston Pork Butt
2 Tbsp Bacon Grease (use butter if necessary)
1 Large Onion sliced
2 Tbsp Cumin
2 Tbsp Thyme
2 Tbsp Chili Powder
1 Tbsp Salt
1 Tbsp Pepper
4 Tbsp Minced Garlic
1 Cup Water

INSTRUCTIONS:

•Use the bacon grease to lightly brush the bottom of the slow cooker.
•Insert the sliced onion and the garlic into the slow cooker.
•Remove the fat from the meat and cut the top of the meat in a crisscross pattern.
•Place the spices in a bowl and mix well.
•Rub the spice mix on the meat ensuring to get the spices into the crisscross marks.
•Place the excess spices over the onion and garlic mix.
•Insert the seasoned meat into the crockpot and pour the water over the meat.
•Place for 8 hours on High until the meat is tender and soft.

Kale and Roasted Red Pepper Frittata

INGREDIENTS:

1 - 2 tsp olive oil to saute the kale
5 oz. baby kale
non-stick spray or oil
6 oz. roasted red pepper (from a jar), diced fairly small
1/4 cup sliced green onion
4-5 oz. crumbled Feta
8 eggs, well beaten
1/2 tsp. Spike Seasoning (or other all-purpose seasoning blend)
fresh-ground black pepper to taste
low-fat sour cream for serving (optional, but good)

INSTRUCTIONS:

•Rinse the baby kale and pat dry using paper towels.
•Pour the oil into a skillet and heat well.
•Toss in the baby kale and saute for about 4 minutes until the kale is soft and tender.
•Spray the slow cooker with a non-stick spray.
•Place the sautéed kale into the slow cooker.
•Toss in the red peppers and green onions into the slow cooker.
•Whisk the eggs in a bowl and pour the egg mixture into the slow cooker.
•Mix all ingredients together.
• Sprinkle the seasonings and the crumbled Feta cheese.
•Leave for about 2-3 hours on low until the frittata is firm and the Feta melted.
•Serve warm with low fat sour cream, if required.

Spicy Mandarin Chicken with Herbs in Crockpot

INGREDIENTS:

For the chicken:
6 chicken thighs
1 Tbsp Chinese Five Spice Powder
1/2 tsp kosher salt
For the sauce:
1 cup no sugar added mandarin orange slices
1 tsp minced garlic
1 Tbsp minced ginger
1/2 tsp sliced red chilis (or red pepper flakes)
1 Tbsp lime juice
1 Tbsp granulated sugar substitute
1 tsp sesame oil
2 Tbsp fish sauce
1/2 tsp xanthan gum

INSTRUCTIONS:

•Mix the spice powder and kosher salt in a bowl.
•Season the chicken pieces with the mix.
•Place the thigh pieces with skin facing the bottom on a heated skillet for about 3-4 minutes.
•Flip the pieces onto the other sides and allow to brown for about 2-3 minutes.
•Lay the browned chicken thighs in the slow cooker.
•Mix all the sauce ingredients (excluding the xanthan gum) in a bowl.
•Toss in the sauce over the chicken thighs.
•Leave on low for about 6 hours or 4 hours on high.
•Transfer the chicken into a platter.
•Pour the sauce into a blender and mix in the xanthan gum.
•Process for about 25 seconds and pour over the thighs.
•Serve warm and garnish with Cilantro if required.

Crockpot Recipe for Beans, Italian Sausage and Greens

INGREDIENTS:

1 cup uncooked dried beans of any type, soaked overnight
1/2 tsp. garlic powder
1/2 tsp. onion powder
4-5 links hot turkey or pork Italian Sausage
1-2 tsp. oil, for browning sausage
1 bunch collard greens, cut into ribbons and washed
1/2 cup bean cooking liquid
1 tsp. finely minced fresh garlic
Parmesan cheese for serving, if desired

INSTRUCTIONS:

•Place the beans in a saucepan with sufficient water to cover the beans.
•Mix in the onion powder and garlic powder and allow the beans to cook for about 25-30 minutes.
•Remove the cooking water, keeping about ½ cup aside for later use.
•While the beans are being cooked, pour a little of the oil into a skillet.
•Heat well and saute the sausages until brown in color.
•Transfer the browned sausages into a chopping board and slice them evenly.
•Remove the stems from the collard green, cut the greens into crosswise ribbons and then into 2-3 sections.
•Rinse the greens and place them in the crockpot.
•Pour the kept aside ½ cup of cooking water into the skillet, add the garlic and cook for about 3 minutes.
•Place the beans and sausages in the crockpot.
•Pour the liquid from the skillet over the ingredients in the crockpot and cook for 2-3 hours on high or 4-6 hours on low until the ingredients are well cooked.
•Serve warm and garnish with Parmesan cheese if required.

Crockpot Spicy Butter Chicken

INGREDIENTS:

2 lbs chicken breast, cubed
1 tbsp vegetable oil
1 shallot, finely chopped
1/4 white onion, chopped
2 tablespoons butter
2 tsp lemon juice
4 garlic cloves, minced
1 inch ginger, minced
2 tsp garam masala
1 tsp chili powder
1 tsp ground cumin
1 bay leaf
1/4 cup plain non fat yogurt
1/4 cup half and half
3/4 cup skim milk
1 cup tomato sauce
2 1/4 teaspoon cayenne pepper, or to taste
1 pinch salt
1 pinch black pepper

INSTRUCTIONS:

•Pour the olive oil into a skillet and heat well.
•Saute the onion and shallot until soft.
•Mix the butter, ginger, lemon juice, garlic, garam masala, chili, cumin, cayenne and bay leaf.
•Leave for about 1-2 minutes.
•Mix in the tomato sauce and leave for about 2-3 minutes.
•Add half the quantities of milk and yogurt and mix well.
•Lower the heat and leave for 8-10 minutes ensuring to stir at internals.
•Adjust seasonings with salt and pepper.
•Place all the ingredients into a food processor and process until the mixture is well combined.
•Mix in the chicken breast cubes into the slow cooker and leave for about 4 hours.
•Serve with cauliflower rice.

Slow Cooker Lemon and Olives Chicken

INGREDIENTS:

2 ribs celery, chopped
1 bulb fennel, cored and chopped
1 onion, chopped
16 large stuffed green olives
4 cloves garlic, crushed
2 bay leaves
½ tsp dried oregano
¼ tsp salt
¼ tsp pepper
12 boneless skinless chicken thighs
¾ cup sodium-reduced chicken broth
¼ cup all-purpose flour
2 tbsp lemon juice
½ cup chopped fresh parsley
Grated zest of 1 Lemon

INSTRUCTIONS:

•Place the carrots, fennel, celery, onion, garlic, olives, bay leaves and oregano in a slow cooker.
•Mix in the salt and pepper.
•Lay the chicken thighs over the vegetables.
•Pour the ¾ cup of water and the broth over the ingredients.
•Place lid, cover and leave the ingredients to cook for about 6 hours.
•Remove the bay leaves from the cooker.
•In a bowl, place the flour, cooking liquid (1 cup) and the lemon juice and whisk well.
•Pour the mixture into the slow cooker and leave until the mixture becomes thick in consistency for about 12-15 minutes.
•Garnish with mixed parsley and lemon zest.
•Serve warm and enjoy.

BBQ Pot Roast with Garlic and Sauce

INGREDIENTS:

8 lb Beef Chuck Shoulder Roast
1 Yellow Onion
5 tsp Minced Garlic
3 T Bacon Grease (can use butter)
2 T Worcestershire Sauce
4 T Vinegar
1 T Yellow Mustard
4 T Splenda
1 tsp Liquid Smoke
To Taste Salt and pepper

INSTRUCTIONS:

•Chop the yellow onion roughly and leave aside.
•Rub the roast with salt and pepper.
•Place the bacon fat in a skillet and heat well.
•Place the seasoned roast on the skillet and brown both sides leaving 1 to ½ minutes per side.
•Insert the browned meat into the crockpot.
•Saute the onions using the same skillet and place on the meat.
•In a bowl, mix the garlic, mustard, Worcestershire, Splenda, vinegar and the liquid smoke.
•Pour the mixture into the crockpot and leave for 1 to 1 1/2 hours for each 1 lb of the meat.
•Transfer the meat into a platter.
•Pour the liquid into a saucepan and leave on the heat until the mixture reduces into half of the quantity.
•Serve over meat.

Chicken Lettuce Wraps

INGREDIENTS:

3 large boneless skinless chicken breasts
1 celery stalk
1 onion, diced
1 clove garlic
16 oz low sodium chicken broth
1/2 cup hot wing sauce
large lettuce leaves (Bibb or iceberg)
1 1/2 cups shredded carrots
2 large celery stalks, thinly sliced
blue cheese, for serving
ranch dressing, for serving

INSTRUCTIONS:

•Place the chicken breasts, celery stalk, diced onion and garlic in a slow cooker.
•Pour the chicken broth over the ingredients into the slow cooker.
•Place lid, cover and leave for 8 hours on low or 4 hours on high.
•Transfer the chicken breasts on to a platter.
•Takeout about ½ cup broth from the slow cooker and remove the balance broth.
•Use a fork to shred the meat and place back again into the slow cooker.
•Add the kept aside broth, sauce and cook for another 30 minutes.
•Serve the meat on lettuce wraps, topped up with the rest of the ingredients.
•If required serve with ranch dressing.

Cheesesteak casserole- low carb

INGREDIENTS:

2 lbs chip steak or 2 lbs cube steaks, cut into strips
1 green pepper, cut into strips
1 red pepper, cut into strips
1 onion, thinly sliced
1/2 lb mushroom, sliced more to taste
1 tablespoon olive oil
3/4 teaspoon kosher salt
3/4-1 teaspoon fresh ground pepper
1/4 lb pepperoni, thinly sliced
8 ounces provolone cheese, thinly sliced

INSTRUCTIONS:

•Pour the olive oil into a skillet.
•Temper the mushrooms until soft and tender for 5-6 minutes.
•Place in the crockpot and add the balance ingredients excluding provolone.
•Leave for 6 hours on low.
•Mix well and transfer into 6 serving bowls.
•Add cooking juices and provolone into each serving bowl.
•Once the cheese is melted serve garnished as required.

Lime and Creamy Chicken in Slow Cooker

INGREDIENTS:

2 cups mild or medium salsa, simmered to reduce to 1 cup
4 boneless, skinless chicken breasts, trimmed and cut in half lengthwise
salt and fresh ground black pepper, for seasoning chicken
2 T fresh-squeezed lime juice (or less if you're not that into lime)
1 cup grated low-fat Mozzarella

INSTRUCTIONS:

•Remove unnecessary and extra fat from the meat and slice each piece into half.
•Spray the slow cooker with a non-stick spray and lay the chicken pieces seasoned with salt and pepper in a slow cooker.
•Add the lime juice to the reduced 1 cup of simmering salsa and pour the warm mixture over the meat.
•Cook for about 60-90 minutes on high until the chicken is cooked but not too tender.
•Spray a casserole dish with a cooking spray and arrange the chicken in the dish.
•Spread the chunky parts of the salsa over the chicken.
•Sprinkle about 1 cup of the Mozzarella over the meat and place the dish under the preheated broiler.
•Leave the dish for about 5 minutes until the cheese melts and become a bubbly brown.
•Serve warm with sour cream and enjoy!

Buffalo Chicken

INGREDIENTS:

2 lbs. boneless, skinless chicken
2 whole carrots
2 whole ribs celery
1 small onion, quartered
2 clove garlic
1.5 cups chicken broth
Salt and pepper
1/2-2/3 cup store bought buffalo sauce
Optional: 2 tbsp. butter, add 1 point per serving

INSTRUCTIONS:

•Place the chicken breast in the crockpot.
•Spread the garlic, carrots, celery ribs, onion and garlic on the meat.
•Pour the broth over the ingredients and adjust seasonings.
•Allow to cook for about 4 hours on high.
•Keep aside 1/3 cup of the mixture and remove the rest of the ingredients including the vegetables.
•Shred the meat, mix in with the buffalo sauce and butter.
•Cook for 15-20 minutes and serve warm.

Juicy Beef shank & Cabbage Stew

INGREDIENTS:

½ pound organic baby carrots
2 medium onions, roughly chopped
1 small cabbage (about 2 pounds), cored, and cut into 8 wedges
8 garlic cloves, peeled and smashed
2 Turkish bay leaves
2 center-cut grass fed beef shanks (about 2" thick)
Kosher salt
Freshly ground pepper
15 ounce can of organic diced tomatoes, drained
1 cup organic chicken broth
2 tablespoons coconut aminos

INSTRUCTIONS:

•Place the carrots, onions, cabbage wedges, garlic and bay leaves in a slow cooker.
•Season the beef with salt and pepper and place them on the vegetables.
•Pour the broth and the diced tomatoes into the slow cooker.
•Cover with lid and cook for about 9 hours on low.
•Remove the meat when cooked and shred with the use of a fork.
•Add the coconut aminos and adjust seasonings to suit your taste.
•Serve warm and enjoy!

Slow Cooker Tomato Chicken Tinga

INGREDIENTS:

2 lbs chicken breast
1/2 large onion, minced
4 cloves garlic, minced
1.5 cups diced tomatoes with green chiles
3 tbsp. chipotle salsa or blended chipotles
1/2 tsp. salt

INSTRUCTIONS:

•Place the chicken breast in the slow cooker.
•Add all other ingredients and mix well.
•Allow the ingredients to cook for about 4 hours on high.
•Transfer the chicken onto a platter and shred using a fork.
•Mix in some juice and tomatoes from the cooked mixture onto the shredded chicken.
•Serve warm and enjoy!

Slow Cooker Dark Chocolate Pepper Chicken Mole

INGREDIENTS:

2 lbs chicken pieces (breasts and legs work well) bone in, Skin removed
salt and pepper
2 tbsp ghee
1 medium onion, chopped
4 cloves garlic, crushed or minced
6 - 7 whole tomatoes, peeled, seeded and chopped
5 dried New Mexico chili peppers, rehydrated and chopped
¼ cup almond butter
2.5 oz dark chocolate (70% or above)
1 teaspoon sea salt
1 teaspoon cumin powder
½ teaspoon cinnamon powder
½ tsp guajillpo chili powder
avocado, cilantro and jalapeno, all chopped.

INSTRUCTIONS:

•Rub the salt and pepper on the chicken pieces.
•Place the ghee on a skillet and heat well.
•Toss in the chicken pieces and allow both sides to brown well.
•Transfer the browned chicken pieces into a slow cooker.
•Place the onion into the same skillet and temper until soft and tender.
•Mix in the crushed or minced garlic and leave for 2 minutes.
•Remove the garlic and onion and insert into the slow cooker.
•Mix in the tomatoes, almond butter, chili peppers and dark chocolate.
•Sprinkle the spices and the salt into the slow cooker.
•Allow to cook for about 4-6 hours on low.
•Place avocado, jalapeno and cilantro on top of the mole and serve.

Greek Stuffed Chicken Breasts with Olives in Slow Coker

INGREDIENTS:

2 lbs. boneless skinless chicken breast (about 6 6oz. chicken breasts)
3 cups finely chopped spinach
2 roasted red peppers, chopped
1/4 cup sliced black olives
1 cup chopped artichoke hearts
4 oz. reduced fat feta
1 tbsp. oregano, chopped
1 tsp. garlic powder
1.5 cups chicken broth
Salt and pepper

INSTRUCTIONS:

•Place the chopped spinach, roasted peppers, artichoke hearts, oregano, feta, garlic powder, salt and pepper in a bowl and mix well.
•Rub the meat pieces with the above mixture and season well.
•Crate a deep slit in the middle of the breast pieces ensuing not to separate the pieces.
•Insert the vegetable mixture into the slits and place in the slow cooker with the stuffed side facing upwards.
•Pour the chicken broth over the breast pieces and allow to cook for 4 hours on low.
•Ensure the chicken is cooked fully prior to serving.

Slow Cooker Roast Tomato Chicken

INGREDIENTS:

4-5 pound organic kosher chicken
2 tablespoons of ghee
2 onions, chopped medium (or 2 cups of your favorite alliums)
6 cloves of garlic, peeled
1 teaspoon tomato paste (you can use up to a tablespoon to add more umami)
¼ cup chicken stock
¼ cup white wine (replace with 1/4 cup extra chicken stock if on Whole30)
Sunny Paris seasoning (or your favorite seasoning)
Kosher salt
Freshly ground pepper

INSTRUCTIONS:

•Place the ghee in a skillet and heat until the ghee is melted.
•Toss in the onions, garlic and tomato paste and leave for about 8-12 minutes.
•Season the chopped vegetables with salt and pepper depending on your taste.
•Pour the wine or chicken stock and deglaze the skillet.
•Transfer the browned ingredients into a slow cooker.
•Season the chicken with salt and pepper and any poultry seasoning of your preference.
•Place the chicken pieces in the slow cooker, cover and cook for about 4-6 hours on low.
•Once the chicken is cooked remove from the slow cooker and allow to cool for about 25 minutes.
•Use your hands and split up the chicken and serve warm with gravy.
•Enjoy!

Crockpot Sunday Chicken Barbacoa

INGREDIENTS:

2 lbs. chicken breast
1/2-1 7 oz. can of chipotles in adobo sauce
4 whole garlic cloves
1 onion, quartered
1/2 tbsp. cumin
1 tsp. oregano
1/2 cup chicken broth
Salt and pepper

INSTRUCTIONS:

•Rub the salt and pepper onto the chicken breast.
•Place the seasoned chicken into the crockpot.
•Toss in the onion, garlic, sauce, cumin and oregano.
•Pour the broth over the ingredients.
•Cook for about 4 hours.
•Remove the cooked onions, garlic and peppers.
•Shred the meat and enjoy!

Crockpot Zucchini Noodles and Cauliflower Bolognese

INGREDIENTS:

For the bolognese:
1 head of cauliflower, cut up into florets
3/4 cup diced red onion
2 small garlic cloves, minced
2 tsp dried oregano flakes
1 tsp dried basil flakes
2 14oz cans diced tomatoes, no salt added
1/2 cup vegetable broth, low-sodium
1/4 tsp red pepper flakes
salt and pepper, to taste
For the pasta:
5 large zucchinis, Blade A

INSTRUCTIONS:

•Mix all the ingredients required for the Bolognese in a bowl.
•Insert the combination into a crockpot.
•Let the ingredients cook for 3 ½ hours on high.
•Once cooked botch the cauliflower using a fork.
•Prepare the zucchini noodles and serve into bowls.
•Lay the Bolognese on top of the zucchini noodles and serve.

Rotisserie Garlic Chicken in Crockpot

INGREDIENTS:

1 3 lb. chicken, cleaned with fat removed
1 tsp. smoked paprika
1/2 tsp. salt
1/2 tsp. pepper
1/2 tsp. garlic powder
1/2 tsp. dried basil
1/2 tsp. dried oregano
1 lemon
Optional: 3-5 small red potatoes (add points based on size)

INSTRUCTIONS:

•Wrap about 5 potatoes with aluminum foil and lay at the bottom of a crockpot.
•Pour the lemon juice into a bowl and mix with the spices.
•Season the chicken with the lemon juice and spice mix.
•Insert the lemon into the cavity of the chicken and place the stuffed chicken on the aluminum wrapped potatoes.
•Allow to cook for 8 hours on low.
•If required, the chicken could be roasted on a preheated oven of 500F for 10-12 minutes for a crispy skin.

Slow Cooker Green Chile Shredded Beef with Fruit Salsa

INGREDIENTS:

2 lb. beef chuck roast, well trimmed and cut into thick strips
1 T Kalyn's Taco Seasoning
2-3 tsp. olive oil
2 cans (4 oz. can) diced green chiles with juice

Ingredients for Cabbage Slaw and Dressing:
1 small head green cabbage
1/2 small head red cabbage
1/2 cup thinly sliced green onion
6 T mayo or light mayo
4 tsp. fresh squeezed lime juice
2 tsp. (or more) Green Tabasco Sauce

Ingredients for the Avocado Salsa:
2 large avocados, diced
1 medium Poblano (Pasilla) pepper, diced very small
1 T fresh-squeezed lime juice
1 T extra-virgin olive oil
1/2 cup finely chopped cilantro

INSTRUCTIONS:

•Remove all unnecessary fat from the roast and cut into strips.
•Season the beef strips with taco seasoning.
•Pour the oil into a skillet and heat well.
•Place the beef onto the heated skillet and brown both sides.
•Place the beef in the slow cooker and add the green chiles and the juice.
•Cook until the meat is tender for about 3-4 hours on High.
•Remove the beef onto a chopping board and shred the meat with a fork.
•Place the shredded meat back again into the slow cooker and keep the mixture warm.
•Slice the cabbage and the green onions into very tiny strips using a slicer.
•Make the dressing by whisking the mayo, green Tabasco sauce and the lime juice together.
•Mix the strips of cabbage and onions with the dressing.
•Slice the avocado and mix with the lime juice.
•Chop the cilantro and Poblano chile and mix with the avocado.

- Pour the olive oil and mix again.
- Place the slaw in a bowl and top up with the beef and avocado salsa.
- Serve with Green Tabasco and enjoy!

Crock Pot Pollo Pibil With Habaneros

INGREDIENTS:

3 lbs boneless, skinless chicken thighs, trimmed of fat
1/2 cup orange juice
2 habaneros, seeded and diced
3 garlic cloves, diced
1 onion, chopped into quarters
1 tbsp coriander
1 tsp cumin
1 tsp dried oregano
4 tbsp Achiote paste
1/4 cup chicken broth
Salt and pepper
1/2 cup apple cider vinegar

INSTRUCTIONS:

•Season the chicken thighs with salt and pepper.
•Place the seasoned thighs in the slow cooker.
•Place the rest of the ingredients in a food processor and process until well blended to make the sauce.
•Pour the sauce over the meat and cook for about 4 hours until the meat is tender.
•Use a fork and shred the meat into pieces.
•Allow the mixture to cook for 25-30 minutes and leave the cover open.
•Once the sauce thickens up pour over the meat.
•Serve with burritos, rice, tacos or baked tortillas.
•Pickled red onions can be served for garnishing purposes.

Crockpot Thai Vegie Curry Chicken

INGREDIENTS:

- 1.5 cans light coconut milk
- 3 tbsp green curry paste
- 3 tbsp brown sugar
- 4 garlic cloves, minced
- 2.5 pounds chicken breast, cut into smaller chunks
- 1 bag stir fry fresh vegetables (or your own combo)
- 1 can baby mini corn, drained
- 1 red onion, sliced
- 2 tbsp cornstarch

INSTRUCTIONS:

- Place the coconut milk, sugar, garlic and curry paste into the slow cooker and whisk well.
- Place the chicken, baby corn, onion and vegetables in the slow cooker.
- Mix in the balance vegetables and leave for 4 hours until all ingredients are cooked through.
- Lastly add the cornstarch and water (2tbsp).
- Leave for about another 20 minutes until the mixture becomes thick in consistency.

Slow Cooker Pepper Jerk Chicken

INGREDIENTS:

1.5 pounds boneless, skinless chicken thighs
1.5 pounds bone-in, skinless chicken breasts
1/4 cup fresh lime juice
4 garlic cloves
2 tbsp fresh thyme
1 tbsp minced fresh ginger
1 tbsp dark brown sugar
2 tsp allspice berries
4 scallions
3-4 habanero peppers, seeded
1.5 tsp salt
2 tbsp white vinegar
1 red pepper
Salt and pepper

INSTRUCTIONS:

•Place all the ingredients excluding the chicken into a blender.
•Place the chicken into the crockpot and pour the mixture over the chicken.
•Leave for about 6 hours, shred the chicken parts into pieces using forks.

Slow Cooker Mandarin Orange Chicken

INGREDIENTS:

For the chicken:
6 chicken thighs
1 Tbsp Chinese Five Spice Powder
1/2 tsp kosher salt

For the sauce:
1 cup no sugar added mandarin orange slices
1 tsp minced garlic
1 Tbsp minced ginger
1/2 tsp sliced red chilis (or red pepper flakes)
1 Tbsp lime juice
1 Tbsp granulated sugar substitute
1 tsp sesame oil
2 Tbsp fish sauce

INSTRUCTIONS:

•Season the chicken pieces with the salt and five spice powder.
•Place the pieces with skin side down on a heated skillet and allow to brown for about 3-4 minutes.
•Flip over the pieces and leave for another 3-4 minutes.
•Insert the browned pieces into the slow cooker, with skin side facing upwards.
•Mix all other ingredients except for the gum in a bowl.
•Pour over the meat and cook for 4 hours on High or 6 hours on low.
•Transfer the cooked chicken pieces into a platter.
•Place the balance sauce into a blender, toss in ½ tsp gum and process for 20-25 seconds.
•Pour over the cooked chicken pieces and garnish with cilantro if required.

Pork Carnitas in Slow Cooker

INGREDIENTS:

2.5 lbs. pork shoulder,lean only, trimmed of fat
1 onion, diced
3-4 garlic cloves, minced
3/4 tsp salt
1/2 tsp. pepper
1 tsp oregano
1 tsp cumin
1-2 diced chipotle peppers and 2 tbsp adobo sauce
3/4 cup light beer or chicken broth
1-2 bay leaves

INSTRUCTIONS:

•Preheat the oven to 500F.
•Rub the pork shoulder with salt and pepper.
•Insert the seasoned pork in a crockpot.
•Mix the balance ingredients and place over the seasoned pork in the crockpot.
•Allow the ingredients to cook on low for about 6-8 hours until the meat is tender.
•Spread the meat on a baking sheet and place in the preheated oven.
•Leave for 5-6 minutes until the meat is crisp around the corners and nicely toasted.
•Enjoy!

Pork Tenderloin with Herbs

INGREDIENTS:

1.5 lb pork tenderloin
1 cup chicken stock
1/2 cup of your favorite salsa
2 tbsp smoked paprika
1 tbsp oregano
1/2 tsp salt
Black pepper

INSTRUCTIONS:

•Place the pork into the crockpot.
•Mix the rest of the ingredients in a bowl and pour over the meat.
•Allow to cook for 4 hours on High.
•Use a fork to shred the meat into pieces.
•Leave in the crockpot for 20-30 minutes until the liquid is absorbed into the pork.
•Serve warm.

Crock Pot Orange flavored Pork Crisp

INGREDIENTS:

3 lbs of pork shoulder, trimmed of fat
1/2 cup orange juice
2 habaneros, seeded and diced
3 garlic cloves, diced
1 onion, chopped into quarters
1 tbsp coriander
1 tsp cumin
1 tsp dried oregano
4 tbsp Achiote paste
1/2 cup chicken broth
Salt and pepper
1/2 cup apple cider vinegar
1/4 cup cilantro for garnish

INSTRUCTIONS:

•Mix the Achiote paste, salt and pepper together in a bowl.
•Rub the pork with the mixture and season well.
•Place the onion pieces and garlic inside the crockpot.
•Insert the seasoned meat into the crockpot and lay over the onions and garlic.
•Cook on low for 6-8 hours until the meat is tender.
•Shred the meat using a fork and mix with the sauce.
•Use chopped cilantro for garnishing and serve with rice or in tacos.

Crockpot Easy Cheeseburger Soup

INGREDIENTS:

1.5 lb ground beef
3 cups beef broth
8 oz. tomato paste
1½ tomatoes, chopped
½ red bell pepper, chopped
3 celery sticks, chopped
½ cup onions, chopped
1½ teaspoons parsley
1 teaspoon Worcestershire sauce
1 teaspoon garlic powder
½ teaspoon salt
½ teaspoon pepper
½ cup of cheese.
2 slices bacon, cooked and chopped (optional)

INSTRUCTIONS:

•Place the beef in a skillet and allow the meat to brown well.
•Remove the excess fat throughout the cooking process.
•Toss in the onions, celery and red pepper.
•Place the beef mixture and the balance ingredients into the slow cooker.
•Combine all ingredients together and more broth could be added if needed.
•Cook on 3-5 hours on High or 6-8 hours on Low.
•Continue to stir the mixture at least 2-3 times.
•Serve garnished with cheese, bacon or mayo if required.

Crock Pot Spicy Pork Adobado

INGREDIENTS:

3 lbs of pork shoulder, trimmed of fat
3 ounces of dried New Mexico Chiles
2 chipotles in adobo
6 garlic cloves
1 onion, chopped into quarters
1 tbsp coriander
1 tsp cumin
1 tsp dried oregano
2 bay leaves
Salt and pepper
1/4 cup cilantro for garnish

INSTRUCTIONS:

•Place the Mexican chiles on a heated skillet and toast for 4-5 minutes until the aroma fills the air and the chiles puffs up.
•Allow to cool, deseed and remove the stem.
•Place the toasted chiles in a saucepan and pour water to cover them.
•Allow the mixture to boil for about 25-30 minutes.
•Mix in the peppers and about 1 cup of the cooking liquid, cumin, chipotles, onion, garlic, coriander and oregano.
•Place them in a blender and process until the mixture is well combined to make the adobo sauce.
•Rub the pork with salt and pepper.
•Pour the thickened sauce into the crockpot and place the seasoned pork over the sauce.
•Cook on low for about 6-8 hours until the meat is nice and tender.
•Shred the pork using two forks and combine well with the sauce.
•Delicious to be served with rice or to be used in tacos.
•Serve garnished with chopped cilantro.

Crock Pot Cheese and Cauliflower Florets

INGREDIENTS:

   1 head cauliflower, cut into florets
   1 can condensed cheddar soup
   1 (5 ounce) can evaporated milk
   ½ teaspoon salt
   ½ teaspoon pepper
   ½ teaspoon paprika
   ¼ cup finely diced onion
   2 cups shredded cheddar

INSTRUCTIONS:

•Spray the crockpot with a non-stick cooking spray.
•Place the cauliflower cut into florets in the crockpot.
•Mix the rest of the ingredients in a saucepan.
•Melt the cheese over a medium heat.
•Spread the mixture over the cauliflower.
•Place lid, cover and leave for the ingredients to cook for 3 to 3 ½ hours on low until the cauliflower is soft and tender.

Roast Tri-Tip Tacos

INGREDIENTS:

8 cloves garlic
1 tbsp. smoked paprika
1 tbsp. ancho chili powder
1 tsp. salt
1 tsp. black pepper
2 lbs. lean tri-tip sirloin roast, trimmed of fat
1 onion, chopped
1 bay leaf
1 cup beef broth

INSTRUCTIONS:

•Place the cloves of garlic in a food processor and process until it forms a paste.
•Mix in the salt, chile powder, paprika and pepper.
•Season the tri-tip with the paste.
•If required, the tri-tip could be grilled as well.
•Place the onions, trip tip in the crockpot and pour the beef broth over the onions.
• Leave for about 8 hours on low until the ingredients are cooked.
•Prior to 30 minutes of cooking time, remove lid and transfer the meat into a platter.
•Shred the tender meat using a fork.
•Cook without the lid for the last 30 minutes.
•Can be served in warm tortillas or wrapped up with lettuce or with rice as required.

Bacon Crockpot Chicken with Sour Cream

INGREDIENTS:

8 bacon slices
8 boneless, skinless chicken breasts
2 (10 oz) cans roasted garlic cream of mushroom soup
1 cup sour cream
1/4 cup flour (all purpose or gluten free blend)
Salt and pepper to taste

INSTRUCTIONS:

•Place the slices of bacon in a skillet and leave on a low heat.
•When the rashers of bacon are pliable drain the oil using paper towels.
•Cover each chicken piece with a slice of bacon and lay in a crockpot.
•Combine the mushroom soup, cream and the flour in a bowl and whisk well.
•Pour the flour mixture over the chicken pieces.
•Place lid and cook for 6-8 hours on low until the mixture is cooked.
•Transfer the cooked chicken into a platter.
•Whisk the sauce inside the crockpot and pour over the chicken.

Slow Cooker Thai Curry Beef

INGREDIENTS:

1 lb. ground beef, 93% lean
1 medium leek, sliced thin
2 garlic cloves, minced
1 tsp. minced ginger
1 tsp. – 1 tbsp. red curry paste
1.5 cups tomato sauce
1 tsp. lime zest
1 tbsp. soy sauce
1/2 cup light coconut milk
2 tsp. lime juice

INSTRUCTIONS:

•Heat a skillet and saute the beef until brown in color.
•Place the meat inside the crockpot and mix in leeks, minced garlic and ginger.
•Mix the curry paste, sauces and lime zest and combine well.
•Cover with lid and allow the ingredients to cook for a little over 4 hours on low.
•Remove the lid and pour in the light coconut milk and the 2 tsp of lime juice.
•Keep for about another 15 minutes to cook and serve.

Ropa Vieja

INGREDIENTS:

1.5 lbs. flank steak, trimmed of fat
1 green pepper
1 yellow pepper
1 onion, sliced thinly
3-4 garlic cloves, minced
1 bay leaves
3/4 tsp. cumin
3/4 tsp. oregano
3/4 cup beef or chicken broth
3 tbsp. tomato paste
1/3 tsp. salt
Optional: 3 tbsp. sliced green olives or 1 tbsp. capers

INSTRUCTIONS:

•Use a cooking spray and slightly spray the crockpot.
•Mix all ingredients together and place in the crockpot.
•Leave the ingredients to cook for about 6 hours on low.
•Serve and enjoy!

Crockpot Lime and Cilantro Chicken

INGREDIENTS:

Chicken Breasts (or a whole chicken or thighs)
5 Limes
Fresh Cilantro
Onion – cubed
Chicken Broth
Salt and Pepper
Garlic Powder

INSTRUCTIONS:

•Place the chicken pieces inside a crockpot.
•Extract the juice from the limes and pour over the chicken pieces along with the broth.
•Season with Salt, pepper and the garlic powder.
•Toss in the cubed onion and some fresh cilantro stalks over the chicken.
•Cook the ingredients for 4-6 hours on low.
•Transfer the meat onto a platter and shred using a fork.
•Remove the cooked cilantro stalks and discard them.
•Place the shredded chicken into the crockpot.
•Mix in more lime juice, broth and fresh cilantro to bring in more flavor.
•Can be served in tortillas with salsa or with salads.

Crockpot Italian Style Beef

INGREDIENTS:

2 lb. boneless beef brisket, trimmed of all fat
1 onion, sliced
4-6 cloves garlic, minced
1 tbsp. dried Italian seasoning
1 tsp red pepper flakes
1/2 cup red wine
2 cups fat free beef broth
Salt and pepper

INSTRUCTIONS:

•Rub salt and pepper on the beef.
•Place the beef in the crockpot along with the rest of the ingredients.
•Cook for 8 hours on low until the beef is tender and can be shredded with ease using a fork.
•Serve and enjoy!

Asian Beef Shred Delight

INGREDIENTS:

3 lbs beef eye of round or bottom round roast, all fat trimmed
1/2 cups soy sauce
1/4 cups rice wine vinegar
1/4 cups brown sugar
2 tbsp ketchup
2 tbsp sesame seeds
1 inch ginger, minced or grated
Optional: 1-3 tsp Asian chili sauce
8 cloves garlic, whole
1/2 red onion, minced
1-2 jalapenos, seeded and minced

INSTRUCTIONS:

•Place the sugar, soy sauce, vinegar, sesame seeds, ginger, ketchup and hot sauce (optional) in a bowl.
•Whisk the ingredients together and mix the onion, garlic and the jalapenos.
•Place the roast in a crockpot and pour the sauce mixture over the meat.
•Cook for 8 hours on low until the beef is very soft and tender.
•Shred the meat with the use of forks and leave for another 25-30 minutes for the liquid to be absorbed into the meat.

Crockpot Beef Ragu with Herbs

INGREDIENTS:

2.5 pounds lean beef chuck, trimmed of fat
1 ribs celery, diced
1/2 onion, diced
1 carrot, peeled and diced
4 garlic cloves, minced
1 14.5 oz can diced tomatoes
1 14.5 oz can crushed tomatoes
1.5 cups beef broth
2 bay leaves
Salt and pepper
2 tbsp fresh rosemary, minced
2 tbsp fresh oregano or thyme, chopped

INSTRUCTIONS:

•Place the diced carrots and celery in a crockpot.
•Mix in the minced garlic and the onion over the carrots.
•Rub salt and pepper on the beef and add to the crockpot with the rest of the ingredients.
•Cook on low for 6-8 hours until the meat is tender.
•Can be served with pasta or polenta.

Spicy Chicken Fajitas

INGREDIENTS:

1 1/2 lb. boneless, skinless chicken breasts
1 large white onion chopped
1 Tbsp. chopped garlic
1tsp. dried oregano
1tsp. chili powder
1 tsp. ground cumin
1/2 tsp. ground coriander
1/2 tsp. kosher salt
1/2 tsp. cayenne pepper
1 can of rotel
Additional Ingredient Options:
Low carb tortillas
Guacamole
Sour Cream
Shredded Cheese
Anything else you like on your fajitas

INSTRUCTIONS:

•Rub salt and pepper on the chicken breasts.
•Add the seasoned meat along with the rest of the ingredients into the crockpot.
•Leave for 4-5 hours on high and remove the meat when tender.
•Cut the meat into strips and enjoy on a tortilla using the rest of the ingredients as desired.

Slow Cooker Hot Roast Machaca

INGREDIENTS:

3 pound beef brisket or lean rump roast, trimmed of fat
Salt and pepper
2 tablespoons Maggi sauce (a Latino seasoning) or 2 tbsp
Worcestershire sauce
4 tablespoons fresh lime juice
1 1/2 cups diced onion
1 cup red bell pepper, diced
3 garlic cloves, minced
3 serrano chiles, stemmed, seeded, and minced
1/2 cup beef broth
1/2 14 oz. can diced tomatoes with juice
1/2 teaspoon dried oregano

INSTRUCTIONS:

•Rub the meat with salt and pepper and place inside the crockpot.
•Place the Maggi in a bowl and pour the broth and the lime juice over it.
•Whisk the mixture well and pour over the seasoned meat in the crockpot.
•Allow to cook for about 8 hours on low until the meat is fork tender.
•Shred the meat using a fork or two and serve.

Slow Cooker Cheesy Fondue

INGREDIENTS:

14 1/2 oz. diced tomatoes, undrained
2/3 c. finely chopped onion
1/2 c. sweet roasted red pepper, finely chopped
4 oz. diced green chilis, undrained
12 oz. Monterey Jack cheese, cubed, with salsa or jalapeno peppers
12 oz. American cheese, cubed
Milk

INSTRUCTIONS:

•Place the tomatoes, peppers and onion in a slow cooker and mix well.
•Toss in the cubed cheese and mix again.
•Cover with lid and allow the mixture to cook on low for about 4 hours or on high for about 2 hours.
•Serve immediately when hot and enjoy.

Beef Tacos in Korean style

INGREDIENTS:

2 pounds beef roast, trimmed of fat
1/2 cup brown sugar (or 1/2 tbsp. molasses and 3.5 tbsp.
Truvia/similar product for lower carb – 5.2 g per serving)
1/3 cup soy sauce
10 cloves of intact garlic
1/2 red onion, diced
2 jalapenos, diced
1 inch fresh ginger root, peeled and grated
2 tablespoons seasoned rice wine vinegar
2 tbsp sesame seeds

INSTRUCTIONS:

•Place the sugar, onion, jalapenos, sesame seeds and ginger in a bowl and mix well.
•Pour the rice vinegar and soy sauce and combine thoroughly to make a sauce.
•Place the beef into the crockpot and mix in the garlic.
•Pour the sauce over the ingredients.
•Allow the mixture to cook on low for about 8-10 hours.
•Prior to 30 minutes of finishing time, shred the meat into pieces.
•Allow the mixture to cook until the sauce is thick in consistency.
•Serve in tortillas garnished with delicious jicama slaw.

Shredded Crock-Pot Chicken

INGREDIENTS:

4 boneless, skinless chicken breasts
1 1/4 teaspoon cumin
1 tablespoon chili powder
1/2 teaspoon coriander
1/4 teaspoon paprika
1 1/2 teaspoon salt
1/2 tsp black pepper
1/3 cup chicken broth
1/3 cup (packed) cilantro leaves, chopped
2 limes
1 large onion, chopped
1 jalapeno, seeded and minced
4 garlic cloves, minced
1 tablespoon olive oil

INSTRUCTIONS:

•Pour the oil into a skillet and heat well.
•Toss in the onion and temper for about 5-6 minutes.
•Mix in the seasonings and spices and leave for another 2-3 minutes.
•Pour the chicken broth and deglaze the skillet to remove any remnants.
•Season the chicken with seasonings and place on the crockpot.
•Drizzle the lime juice and add the jalapeno and cilantro and mix well.
•Pour the onion mixture on top of the ingredients and leave for 3-5 hours on low.
•Transfer the cooked meat, shred and leave aside.
•Spoon the onion mixture over the meat.
•Serve in tortillas with avocado, lettuce, tomato, cilantro, onion and cheese.
•Can be eaten with sour cream and salsa as required.

Crockpot Baby Back Ribs in BBQ Sauce

INGREDIENTS:

1 rack of baby back pork ribs
1 TBSP Splenda
1 tsp chili powder (or more if you like it spicy)
1 TBSP garlic powder
2 tsp celery seed
1 TBSP onion powder
1 TBSP dried oregano
2 tsp Cajun seasoning
1 tsp black pepper
1/4 cup LC BBQ sauce

INSTRUCTIONS:

•Slice the pork ribs into 4 pieces and place in the crockpot.
•Place the rest of the ingredients except the BBQ sauce in a bowl and mix thoroughly.
•Season the sliced ribs with the mixture and cook for about 6 hours on low.
•Splash the BBQ sauce over the ribs and leave the ingredients to cook for further 2-3 hours if necessary.

Melted Ranch Mushrooms

INGREDIENTS:

1 pound fresh mushrooms
1/2 cup butter, melted
1 envelope Ranch salad dressing mix

INSTRUCTIONS:

•Melt the butter and combine with the salad dressing mix.
•Place the fresh mushrooms inside the crockpot.
•Pour the butter mixture over the ingredients.
•Cook for 3-4 hours on low.
•The mixture should be moist and juicy.
•If the ingredients are dry, mix in some water and enjoy.

Cabbage Soup and Sausage Crock Pot

INGREDIENTS:

2 cups potatoes, cubed and peeled
4 cups cabbage and carrot coleslaw mix (packaged)
1 large onion, chopped
2 teaspoons caraway seeds, crushed
1 lb Polish sausage, cooked, halved lengthwise and cut into 1/2 inch slices
4 cups fat free chicken broth

INSTRUCTIONS:

•Place the dry ingredients in the crockpot.
•Pour the chicken broth over the ingredients.
•Cook for about 10-12 hours on low or 5-6 hours on high.
•Serve in soup bowls and enjoy!

Crock-Pot Creamy Chicken Alfredo

INGREDIENTS:

Fresh Boneless Skinless Chicken Breasts (~3.5lbs)
8oz Heavy Whipping Cream
1 Jar Prego Artisan Three Cheese Alfredo
Broccoli

INSTRUCTIONS:

•Place the chicken breasts inside the crockpot.
•Place the cream and cheese Alfredo in a bowl and combine well.
•Pour the mixture over the breasts sufficiently enough to cover the pieces.
•Allow the mixture to cook on high for about 4-5 hours until tender.
•Remove the meat and shred using a fork.
•Serve warm with steamed broccoli.
•Enjoy.

Slow cooker Balsamic Glazed Pork

INGREDIENTS:

Pork
2 ½ pound boneless pork loin roast, trimmed of large fat pockets
1 tsp. poultry seasoning
1 tsp. kosher salt
1/2 tsp. pepper
1 clove garlic, finely minced
1/2 c. water
Balsamic Glaze
1 c. brown sugar
2 T. cornstarch
2/3 c. balsamic vinegar
1 c. water
1/4 c. soy sauce

INSTRUCTIONS:

•Season the pork with seasoning, salt, pepper and garlic.
•Place the seasoned pork in the slow cooker.
•Pour the 1 cup of water around the ingredients and cook for 6-8 hours on low ensuring to cover the slow cooker.
•Whisk the sugar, vinegar, water, cornstarch and the soy sauce in a saucepan and heat well.
•Allow the mixture to simmer until thick in consistency for about 10-12 minutes.
•Transfer the meat onto a platter and shred into pieces.
•Sprinkle the glaze over the pork and serve.

Creamy Bacon Crock Pot Chicken

INGREDIENTS:

8 bacon slices
8 boneless, skinless chicken breasts
2 (10 oz) cans roasted garlic cream of mushroom soup
1 cup sour cream
½ cup flour

INSTRUCTIONS:

You can prepare this one of two ways. Place the bacon in a large skillet and cook over medium-low heat until some of the fat is rendered. Be sure that the bacon is still pliable and not crisp. Drain on paper towels. If you use this method, reduce the flour to ¼ cup. Or don't cook the bacon and proceed with the recipe.Then wrap one slice of bacon around each boneless chicken breast and place in a 4-5 quart crockpot. In medium bowl, combine condensed soups, sour cream, and flour and mix with wire whisk to blend. Pour over chicken. Cover crockpot and cook on low for 6-8 hours until chicken and bacon are thoroughly cooked. You may want to remove the chicken and beat the sauce with a wire whisk so it is very well blended. Pour sauce over chicken. Serves 8 If you have a new hot cooking crockpot, check the chicken at 5 hours. It should be 160 degrees F.

Spring BBQ Ribs in Crockpot

INGREDIENTS:

1 lb Fresh Pork Ribs
35g Tomato Puree (approx 1.5oz)
60ml water (approx 1/4 cup)
15ml Vinegar (approx 1/8 cup)
2 TBSP Worcestershire Sauce
1 TBSP Dry Mustard
1 TBSP Chilli Powder
2 TBSP Splenda

INSTRUCTIONS:

•Coat a skillet with a cooking spray and heat the ribs until each side is well browned.
•Spray the slow cooker with the cooking spray and place the browned ribs in the slow cooker.
•Mix the rest of the ingredients in a bowl and pour the mixture over the ribs.
•Toss the ribs in the mixture to season well.
•Cook for about 8 hours on low.
•Remove from slow cooker and serve warm.

Slow cooker Coconut Lemongrass Pork

INGREDIENTS:

2-3 lb Pork Loin or Butt Roast
2 inch ginger cut into ¼" thick rounds
2-3 cloves garlic minced
2 tsp kosher salt
3 TB olive oil
5 TB minced lemongrass
1 TB apple cider vinegar
1 tsp ground pepper
1 onion sliced into ¼" rounds
½ can coconut milk

INSTRUCTIONS:

•Remove the unnecessary and excess fat from the Butt roast leaving a little fat intact.
•Mark a crisscross pattern on the fat layer on top of the pork.
•Lay the sliced onion rounds in the slow cooker.
•In a separate bowl, mix the garlic, salt, lemongrass, vinegar, pepper and the olive oil to form a paste.
•Season the pork with the paste and place the seasoned pork in the slow cooker.
•Cover and leave overnight for better seasoning.
•In the morning, add the coconut milk and turn the slow cooker into low.
 •Leave for about 8 hours until the meat is tender.
•Shred the meat with a fork and serve warm.

Bone Broth Relish in Crockpot

INGREDIENTS:

1 lb-2 lbs bones from pastured animals
(chicken feet/necks or beef bones knuckles are best)
4 cloves organic garlic
1-2 gallons filtered water
Sea salt and pepper to taste
2 tbsp apple cider vinegar
other of choice vegetables (optional, can make it bitter)
Other herbs (optional)

INSTRUCTIONS:

•Place all the ingredients overnight in a crockpot for about 8-24 hours on low.
•Strain the liquid and place in separate containers.
•Refrigerate until chilled.
•Remove the excess fat and keep aside later for other uses.
•Enjoy the broth or serve to guests.

Slow Cooker Autumn Stew

INGREDIENTS:

2 kg oxtail or beef suitable for slow-cooking (bones included, 2 kg / 4.4 lb / 70 oz), this will yield about 50% meat
1 tbsp ghee, butter or lard
2 cups beef stock, vegetable stock or water
1 red onion
1 garlic head
1 carrot
2 celery stalks
Juice and peel from 1 average orange
1 cinnamon stick
1/4 tsp nutmeg
5-8 cloves
1 star anise
2 bay leaves (fresh or dried)
Freshly ground black pepper to taste
1/2 tsp salt or more to taste
4 heads small lettuce or 2 of medium lettuce

INSTRUCTIONS:

•Preheat the oven to 300F.
•Rub the meat with salt and pepper.
•Heat a skillet with ghee and place the ox tail and heat well.
•Leave the ox tail to brown on both sides and transfer the browned oxtail on a baking tray.
•Slice the onion, extract the juice from the orange, peel the carrots and slice the garlic.
•Mix all the spices in a saucepan and cook for about 5-6 minutes.
•Remove from the heat and leave aside.
•Place the ingredients in the saucepan on the surface of the oxtail and cook for 4 hours until the meat is soft and tender.
•Take out from the oven and leave for a few minutes.
•Remove the spices, vegetables and the orange.
•Shred the tender meat and pour the sauce over the meat.
•Serve on top of lettuce leaves and enjoy.

Slow Cooker Chicken and Sausage Surprise

INGREDIENTS:

1 1/2 lbs boneless skinless chicken breasts
1 package andoulle sausage
1 8 oz package cream cheese, room temperature
1 cup chicken stock
1/2 cup white wine (you can also sub this with beer or chicken stock)
3 gloves of garlic minced
1 small yellow onion diced
2 tbs grainy mustard
1/2 tsp salt
Scallions for garnish
Serve over white rice or buttered noodles

INSTRUCTIONS:

•Place the sausages and chicken in a crockpot.
•Combine the cream cheese, stock, salt, mustard, garlic and wine in a bowl.
•Toss in the onions on top of the sausages and chicken and pour the cheese mix over the onions.
•Place lid, cover and cook for 4 hours on high.
•Check constantly and if too thick, add more broth or wine.
•Adjust seasonings and serve with rice or pasta.

Poached Salmon Spirit

INGREDIENTS:

2 cups water
1 cup dry white wine
1 lemon, thinly sliced
1 shallot, thinly sliced
1 bay leaf
5-6 sprigs fresh herbs, such as tarragon, dill, and/or Italian parsley
1 teaspoon black peppercorns
1 teaspoon kosher salt
2 pounds skin-on salmon (or 4-6 fillets), preferably farm-raised

INSTRUCTIONS:

•Mix the lemon, shallots, herbs, bay leaf, pepper corns and salt in the slow cooker.
•Pour the wine and water over the ingredients.
•Cook for about 30 minutes on high.
•Rub salt and pepper on top of the salmon and place the fish with skin side facing down.
•Place lid, cover and leave the salmon to cook for over 1 hour until the flesh flakes out easily.
•Sprinkle with olive oil and salt.
•Best served with lemon wedges.

Crockpot Sweet Potato Breakfast Pie

INGREDIENTS:

8 eggs, whisked
1 sweet potato or yam, shredded
1lb US Wellness Meats Pork Sausage, broken up
1 yellow onion, diced
1 tablespoon garlic powder
2 teaspoons dried basil
Salt and pepper, to taste
Any extra veggies you want to put in there: peppers, squash, etc.

INSTRUCTIONS:

•Grease the crockpot using a cooking spray or oil to avoid any eggs sticking to the bottom.
•Place all the ingredients in the crockpot, mix well and cook for about 6-8 hours on slow.
•Slice the pie into pieces and serve with vegies of your choice.

Caribbean Ginger Oxtails

INGREDIENTS:

2 lb (1 kg) beef oxtails
2 onions, diced
2 carrots, diced
4 garlic cloves, minced
1 inch piece of ginger, peeled and minced
1 jalapeño pepper, minced (optional)
2 cups beef stock, homemade or organic is best
3 Tablespoons tomato paste
1 Tablespoon allspice berries (or 1 teaspoon ground allspice)
1 teaspoon fish sauce
4 sprigs of fresh thyme (or 1 teaspoon dried thyme)
Coconut oil or fat of choice
Sea salt and pepper

INSTRUCTIONS:

•Pour the coconut oil into a skillet and heat well.
•Rub the oxtails with seasonings and brown the meat on both sides.
•Place the browned meat in the crockpot.
•Toss in the onion, garlic, carrot, ginger and jalapeno into the heated skillet and leave for 5 minutes.
•Pour the stock and add the tomato paste, berries, thyme and fish sauce into the skillet.
•Remove the skillet from the heat and transfer the ingredients into the crockpot to cover the meat.
•Cover and cook for about 6 hours on high.

Easy Short Ribs in Korean Style

INGREDIENTS:

½ c. coconut aminos OR organic Tamari (soy) sauce
⅓ c. Swerve, Confectioners
(Or equivalent)
¼ c. rice vinegar
2 cloves garlic, peeled and smashed
1 TBS grated fresh ginger
½ tsp crushed red pepper
8 (4 lbs) grass fed beef short ribs
1 green cabbage, quartered
½ tsp guar gum (thickener)
1 TBS sesame oil
4 scallions, thinly sliced

INSTRUCTIONS:

•Place the coconut aminos, sauce, sweetener, garlic, ginger, red pepper and vinegar in a slow cooker and mix well.
•Insert the ribs and lay the quartered cabbage pieces on top.
•Cover and cook for 8 hours until the meat is fork tender.
•Transfer the ribs into a platter along with the cabbage.
•Skim the extra fat with the use of a spoon from the liquid and mix in the guar gum dissolved in 1 tbsp of water.
•Leave for about 3 minutes until the sauce thickens and mix in the sesame oil.
•Pour the thick sauce over the ribs and cabbage pieces.
•Serve sprinkled with scallions.

Slow Cooker Spicy Swiss Steak

INGREDIENTS:

A couple of twists of ground pepper (roughly a teaspoon)
1/2 teaspoon Kosher salt
2-1/2 pounds boneless round steak
1 14-1/2 oz can Ro*Tel tomatoes
1 tablespoon liquid smoke, mesquite flavor
1-1/3 cups beef broth
1 cup sliced celery
1/2 cup sliced onions
1/2 cup sliced carrots
1/2 cup bell pepper
2 peeled and minced garlic cloves

INSTRUCTIONS:

•Place all the ingredients into a slow cooker.
•Allow the ingredients to cook for about 8-10 hours on low.
•Ensure the steak is well cooked and serve with salads or vegies of your choice.

Slow cooker Kale and Chicken Soup

INGREDIENTS:

6 boneless, skinless chicken thighs
3 1/2 cups of homemade chicken bone broth
1/2 of a large white onion - chopped
4 large cloves of garlic - smashed
1 1/2 cups shredded carrots
4 cups of chopped kale
1 1/2 tsp. parsley
Salt and pepper to taste

INSTRUCTIONS:

•Place the chicken pieces in the slow cooker and top up with the chopped onions.
•Toss in the garlic and pour the broth around the ingredients.
•Allow to cook for about 6 hours on low until the chicken is fork tender.
•Shred the meat with a fork.
•Toss in the carrots, parsley, and kale and adjust seasonings with salt and pepper.
•Cook for another hour or a little more.
•Enjoy!

Slow Cooker Onions with Coconut Aminos

INGREDIENTS:

4 (or 5) large onions
4 Tbsp butter, cut into pieces or coconut oil
1/4 cup coconut aminos (a soy sauce substitute)
Salt and pepper, to taste

INSTRUCTIONS:

•Chop the large onions into about ¼" pieces and place in the slow cooker.
•Spread the butter and the aminos on top.
•Cook for about 6-8 hours on low.
•Can be served as a side dish or with grilled pork chops or chicken.

Mexican Slow Cooker Chicken

INGREDIENTS:

1 cup sour cream
1/2 cup chicken stock
1 - 14 oz can diced tomatoes and green chilies
1 batch homemade taco seasoning
2 lbs chicken breast

INSTRUCTIONS:

•Pour the sour cream and the chicken stock into the slow cooker.
•Toss in the tomatoes and green chilies and the seasoning.
•Add the chicken breast and mix well.
•Place the lid, cover and cook for about 6-8 hours on low until the ingredients are cooked through.

Slow Cooker Greek Garlic Chicken

INGREDIENTS:

3-4 boneless, skinless chicken breasts
3 Tbsp. Greek Rub I use The Pampered Chef brand
1 1/2 Tbsp. minced garlic
3 Tbsp. lemon juice
1 1/2 cups hot water
2 chicken bullion cubes

INSTRUCTIONS:

•Spray the slow cooker using a cooking spray.
•Season each chicken piece by marinating with the Greek Rub.
•Spread about ½ tbsp. of minced garlic on each chicken piece and place in the slow cooker.
•Splash the lemon juice over the chicken.
•Dissolve the chicken bullion cubes with hot water and pour over the meat.
•Place lid, cover and cook for 6 hours on low until the meat is tender.

Slow Cooker Roast Mix

INGREDIENTS:

3-4 lb roast
3 tsp salt
3 tsp garlic powder
3 tsp onion powder
8 Tbs butter
1 cup water

INSTRUCTIONS:

•Place the roast, salt and the seasonings in the slow cooker.
•Pour the water around the ingredients.
•Lay blobs of butter on the surface.
•Cook the ingredients for about 6 hours on low.

Slow Cooker Peppered Beef Rags

INGREDIENTS:

3 pounds chuck arm pot roast
2 teaspoons granulated garlic
1 teaspoon onion powder
1/2 tablespoon kosher salt
1/2 tablespoon fresh ground black pepper
2 tablespoons Worcestershire Sauce
1 cup cabernet sauvignon—or dry red wine (screw-top is fine)
1/2 tablespoon Country Dijon Mustard
3 tablespoons unfiltered extra virgin olive oil

INSTRUCTIONS:

•Rub the roast with garlic, onion powder, salt and black pepper.
•Place ½ of the olive oil and heat a Dutch oven until well heated over a medium heat.
•Allow the seasoned meat to brown on both sides for 4 minutes on each side.
•Add the balance olive oil half way through the browning process.
•Add the mustard and the red wine and the Worcestershire sauce when the meat is sufficiently browned.
•Allow to cook for about 6 hours in a preheated oven (275F) until the meat is fork tender.
•Transfer the meat from the oven and mix in a bit of gooey fat.
•Shred the meat and place it back again to the pan and mix well with the sauces.

Slow Cooker Whole Garlic Chicken

INGREDIENTS:

1 (5 lbs.) fresh Whole Chicken
1 medium Onion
2 clove Garlic
11 baby Carrot
3 Bay Leaves
½ tbsp. Whole Black Pepper
1 pinch Sea Salt
½ teaspoon celery salt
½ teaspoon garlic powder
½ teaspoon onion powder
1 teaspoon parsley flakes
½ cup Water

INSTRUCTIONS:

•Place the seasonings, spices and parsley flakes in a bowl and mix well.
•Rub the mixture over the chicken.
•Place the vegetables and seasoned chicken in the slow cooker.
•Pour the water around the meat.
•Cook on low for about 7-8 hours until the meat is cooked.
•Transfer the tender meat into a platter.
•Allow to cool for about 5 minutes and slice into pieces as required.
•Serve with salads and enjoy!

Autumn Chili Onion Slow Cooker

INGREDIENTS:

2 1/2 lbs. Lean Ground Beef
1 Medium Red Onion – Chopped – Divided
4 Tbs. Minced Garlic
3 Large Ribs of Celery – Diced
¼ Cup Jalapeno Slices
1 – 6 oz. Can Tomato Paste
1 – 14.5 oz. Can Tomatoes and green chilies
1 – 14.5 oz. Can Stewed Tomatoes with Mexican Seasoning
2 Tbs. Worcestershire Sauce
4 Tbs. Chili Powder
2 1/2 Tbs. Cumin – Mounded
2 tsp. Salt
1/2 tsp. Cayenne
1 tsp. Garlic Powder
1 tsp. Onion Powder
1 tsp. Oregano
1 tsp. Black Pepper
1 Bay Leaf
(2 Tbs. Peace and Love)

INSTRUCTIONS:

•Mix the beef, half the quantity of onions, 2 tbsp of garlic and seasonings together and place on a heated skillet.
•Allow the meat to brown on both sides and remove the excess fat from the skillet.
•Transfer the browned meat and the ingredients to a slow cooker.
•Add the balance ingredients and combine all ingredients until well blended.
•Cook for about 8 hours on low until the meat is tender.
•Serve warm.

Orange and Coconut Aminos Chicken

INGREDIENTS:

¼ cup melted coconut oil
¼ cup coconut milk
2 TBS Swerve Confectioners
1 tsp toasted sesame oil
1 tsp coconut aminos or organic Tamari sauce (soy sauce)
½ tsp freshly grated ginger
½ tsp toasted sesame seeds
½ tsp orange oil/extract
¼ tsp fish sauce (for Umami: see below)
1½ pounds chicken legs or thighs
GARNISH:
1 TBS black sesame seeds
4 green onions, sliced

INSTRUCTIONS:

•Combine the sauce ingredients together in a bowl and mix well until smooth in consistency.
•The sauce once prepared may separate if it is kept for too long.
•Warm gently and whisk well to combine the sauce again.
•Place the chicken legs or thighs in a baking dish and pour the sauce over the meat.
•Cover the meat with an aluminum foil and bake in a preheated oven (375F) for about 45-50 minutes.
•Best to serve with pasta or Quest pasta as required.

Crockpot Jambalaya Tomato Pepper Soup

INGREDIENTS:

5 c. chicken stock.
4 peppers – any color you want, chopped
1 large onion, chopped
1 large can of organic diced tomatoes (leave the juice)
2 cloves garlic, diced
2 bay leafs
1 lb large shrimp, raw and de-veined.
4 oz. chicken, diced
1 pkg spicy Andouille sausage
1/2-1 head of cauliflower
2 c. okra (optional)
3 tbsp Cajun Seasoning
1/4 c. Frank's Red Hot (or hot sauce of your choice)
*How to Make Your Own Cajun Seasoning (from Emeril!):
2 1/2 tablespoons paprika
2 tablespoons salt
2 tablespoons garlic powder
1 tablespoon black pepper
1 tablespoon onion powder
1 tablespoon cayenne pepper
1 tablespoon dried oregano
1 tablespoon dried thyme
(Yields about 2/3 c.)

INSTRUCTIONS:

•Place the peppers, chopped onions, garlic, chicken, seasoning, Red Hot and bay leaves in the crockpot.
•Pour the broth over the ingredients.
•Cook for about 6 hours on low and just 30 minutes prior to finishing time toss in the sausages.
•Prepare the cauliflower rice by placing the cauliflower in a food processor and pulsing until it becomes rice consistency.
•During the last 25 minutes toss in the cauliflower rice and the shrimp.
•Serve and enjoy!

Energetic Slow Cooker Beef Stew

INGREDIENTS:

2 lbs. Stew Beef
3 Tbs. Olive Oil
2 Cups Organic Beef Stock
12 oz. Package Bacon – Cooked Crisp and Crumbled
14.5 oz. Can Organic Diced Tomatoes – Juice Drained
4 oz. Mixed Bell Peppers – Chopped
4 oz. Mushrooms – Quartered
2 Ribs Celery – Chopped
1 Large Carrot – Chopped
1 Small Onion – Chopped
4 Large Cloves Garlic – Minced
2 Tbs. Organic Tomato Paste
2 Tbs. Worcestershire Sauce or Coconut Aminos
2 tsp. Sea Salt
1 ½ tsp. Black Pepper
1 tsp. Garlic Powder
1 tsp. Onion Powder
1 tsp. Dried Oregano
(2 Tbs. Peace and Love)

INSTRUCTIONS:

•Pour the olive oil into a skillet, heat and brown the beef on both sides.
•Remove the browned meat and place in the slow cooker.
•Mix in the stock, tomatoes, bacon, peppers, mushrooms, carrot, celery, onion, tomato paste, garlic, sauce, salt, pepper, garlic and onion powders and oregano.
•Cover and allow to cook for about 6-8 hours.

Tender Braised Cabbage with Bacon

INGREDIENTS:

1 head green cabbage
1 large sweet onion, halved and sliced
4 garlic cloves, coarsely chopped -optional
1/4 cup bacon fat, melted
1/4- 1/2 cup bone broth, wine or water
Smoked coarse sea salt or coarse celtic sea salt
Caraway seeds -optional

INSTRUCTIONS:

•Place the bacon fat in the crockpot.
•Add the sliced onion and leave for a few minutes on high.
•Separate the cabbage into 12 pieces and place on the onion.
•Pour the bone broth/wine/water and mix in the salt and the caraway seeds (optional).
•Cook the ingredients for about 1 hours on high.
•If required add more broth as necessary.
•Allow to cook for about another 4 -5 hours.
•Sprinkle with vinegar and adjust seasonings.

Crock-Pot Lobster and Tomato Mix

INGREDIENTS:

2 Shallots, Finely Minced
1 Clove Garlic, Finely Minced
2 (14.5 Oz.) Cans Petite Diced Tomatoes, With Juice
1 (32 Oz.) Carton Low-Sodium Chicken Broth
1 Tablespoon Old Bay Seasoning
1 Teaspoon Dried Dill
1/4 Cup Fresh Parsley, Chopped
1 Teaspoon Freshly Cracked Black Pepper
1/2 Teaspoon Paprika
4 Lobster Tails
1 Pint Heavy Cream

INSTRUCTIONS:

•Saute the garlic and shallots in a skillet and transfer the mixture to a crockpot.
•Toss in the tomatoes, seasoning, dill, parsley, pepper, paprika and the broth.
•Add the lobsters after striking off the fan part from each lobster using a knife.
•Cover and cook for about 6 hours on low.
•Set aside the lobster ends and discard them.
•Add the soup mixture into a blender and puree until smooth.
•Place the soup mixture back again into the crockpot.
•Toss in the tails to the slow cooker and cook for about 45-50 minutes on low.
•Take out the tails from the soup and allow to cool.
•Mix with cream and enjoy!

Chicken Chili and Garlic Soup

INGREDIENTS:

2 Tablespoons Unsalted Butter
1 Onion
1 Pepper
8 Boneless Chicken Thighs (~55 Oz)
8 Slices of Bacon
1 Tablespoon Thyme
1 teaspoon salt
1 teaspoon pepper
1 Tablespoon Minced Garlic
1 Tablespoon Coconut Flour
3 Tablespoons Lemon Juice
1 Cup Chicken Stock
¼ Cup Unsweetened Coconut Milk
3 Tablespoons Tomato Paste

INSTRUCTIONS:

•Slice the onion into thin slices and chop the peppers into fine pieces.
•Place 2 tbsp of the unsalted butter in a crockpot.
•Insert the onion and pepper pieces into the crockpot.
•Place the chicken thighs on the vegetables.
•Slice the bacon into pieces and lay over the chicken thighs.
•Add the coconut flour, garlic and adjust seasonings with salt and pepper.
•Pour the stock, coconut milk and lemon juice over the ingredients.
•Finally add the tomato paste and mix the ingredients together.
•Allow the mixture to cook for about 6-7 hours on low.
•Stir the mixture occasionally.
•Flake the chicken prior to serving.
•Ideal to serve garnished with grated cheese and sour cream.

Chorizo, Chicken and Tomato Soup

INGREDIENTS:

4 Lbs Boneless Skinless Chicken Thighs
1 Lb Chorizo
4 Cups Chicken Stock
1 Cup Heavy Cream
1 Can Stewed Tomatoes
2 Tbsp Minced Garlic
2 Tbsp Worcestershire Sauce
2 Tbsp Frank's Red Hot Sauce
Garnish with Shaved Parmesan and Sour Cream

INSTRUCTIONS:

•Heat a skillet and place the chorizo on the warm skillet.
•Sauté the chorizo for a little while until slightly brown in color.
•Place the chicken thighs in the bottom of a crockpot.
•Lay the browned chorizo over the thighs.
•Toss in the balance ingredients.
•Leave for about 3 hours on high and allow the ingredients to cook well.
•Transfer the chicken thighs into a platter and shred the meat.
•Place the meat back into the crockpot.
•Leave for about 30-40 minutes on a low heat.
•Serve garnished with Parmesan and Sour cream.

Green Chile with Garlic flavor Chicken Recipe

INGREDIENTS:

Crockpot
6 – 8 Boneless Skinless Chicken Thighs, thawed
One 4 oz. Can Green Chiles
2 tsp. Garlic Salt
Optional: Add in 1/2 cup Diced Onions for some extra flavor!

INSTRUCTIONS:

•Place the chicken in a crockpot and cook for about 3 hours on high.
•After the cooking time is completed remove the liquid from the crockpot.
•Add the chiles and salt and mix on to the chicken.
•Leave for another 30 minutes.
•Shred the chicken with a fork and serve in tacos.

Crockpot Stuffed Poblano Peppers with Cauliflower

INGREDIENTS:

1 poblano pepper
1/3 cup finely chopped cauliflower
1/3 lb ground beef
1 tablespoon chopped onion
3 tablespoons tomato sauce

INSTRUCTIONS:

•Heat a skillet and brown the beef and onion ensuring to brown the beef on both sides.
•Combine the beef mix, tomato sauce and cauliflower together and stuff the peppers.
•Pour about ½" water or tomato juice into a slow cooker.
•Insert the stuffed peppers and cook until the peppers are cooked for about 4 hours.

Gizzard and Cilantro Recipe

INGREDIENTS:

1 bunch of organic cilantro, washed and cleaned from stems
3 large cloves of organic garlic, peeled and sliced
1 small organic onion
1 pound of free range chicken gizzards
¼ cup Passata di Pomodoro
½ cup white wine
¼ cup water
A good pinch of celtic sea salt

INSTRUCTIONS:

•Place all the ingredients in a slow cooker and mix well.
•Cook for about 6 hours on low.
•Best served with cassava flour or cauliflower rice.

Slow Cooker Chocolate Cake with a Difference

INGREDIENTS:

1 & 1/2 cups almond flour
3/4 cup Swerve Sweetener
2/3 cup cocoa powder
1/4 cup unflavoured whey protein powder
2 tsp baking powder
1/4 tsp salt
1/2 cup butter, melted
4 large eggs
3/4 cup almond or coconut milk, unsweetened
1 tsp vanilla extract
1/2 cup Sugar-Free Chocolate Chips (optional)

INSTRUCTIONS:

•Grease the slow cooker using a cooking spray.
•Place the almond flour, cocoa powder, sweetener, protein powder, baking powder and salt in a bowl and whisk well.
•Whisk the eggs and add along with butter, vanilla and almond milk.
•Combine the mixture well and toss in the chocolate chips (optional)
•Place the mixture in the greased slow cooker and leave to cook for 3 hours on low.
•Switch off the slow cooker and allow to cook for about 30 minutes.
•Slice the cake into pieces and serve with whipped cream.

Pork In Creamy Dijon Sauce

INGREDIENTS:

1 tablespoon extra-virgin olive oil or more as needed
2½ pounds whole pork tenderloins
Garlic salt and black pepper to taste
¼ teaspoon garlic powder or to taste
1 onion chopped
1 (8 ounce) package sliced fresh mushrooms
½ teaspoon garlic salt
¼ cup white wine
¾ cup heavy cream
¼ cup chicken broth
3 tablespoons Dijon mustard
¼ cup sour cream

INSTRUCTIONS:

•Place the olive oil in a skillet and heat well.
•Rub the pork with the seasonings and garlic power.
•Saute the meat and brown the pork on both sides leaving each side for about 5 minutes.
•Transfer the browned meat onto a platter and keep aside.
•Cook the onion and sliced mushrooms using the same skillet for about 4-5 minutes until soft.
•Transfer the ingredients to the slow cooker and insert the browned meat on top.
•Deglaze the skillet using white wine and add the heavy cream, garlic salt and the broth.
•Leave for 20 minutes until the mixture is thick in consistency.
•Mix in the sour cream and the mustard and leave for a few minutes.
•Spread the thick sauce over the meat.
•Place lid and cook for about 6-7 hours until the meat is soft and tender.

Beef and Cheese Casserole

INGREDIENTS:

- 1/2 pound corned beef diced
- 1 can sauerkraut drained
- 2 cups Swiss cheese shredded
- 1/2 cup mayonnaise
- 1* 8 oz package cream cheese
- 1/2 cup low-sugar ketchup
- 2 tablespoons pickle brine
- 1/2 teaspoon caraway seeds

INSTRUCTIONS:

- Preheat the oven to 350F.
- Melt the cheese, ketchup and the mayonnaise in a skillet over a low heat.
- Mix the sauerkraut, 1 ½ cups of the Swiss cheese and corned beef once the cheese mixture is melted.
- Combine the mixture well.
- Remove the sauce and mix in the pickle brine, 1 tbsp of salt, 1 tsp of vinegar and a dash of garlic salt.
- Grease a pie pan and pour the mixture into the pan.
- Top up with the balance Swiss cheese and garnish with caraway seeds.
- Leave in the oven for about 25 minutes until the cheese becomes bubbly and fully melted.

Garlic Pork Shoulder in Crockpot

INGREDIENTS:

1 teaspoon garlic powder
1 teaspoon ground cumin
1/2 teaspoon crumbled dried oregano
1/2 teaspoon ground coriander
1/4 teaspoon ground cinnamon
1 (4 pound) boneless pork shoulder roast
2-3 bay leaves
2 cups chicken broth

INSTRUCTIONS:

•Place about 2-3 bay leaves in a crockpot.
•Combine all the spices together and rub about ½ of the quantity on one side of the meat.
•Place the seasoned side facing down and toss in the balance spices on the top.
•Pour the broth around the meat and cook for about 5 hours on low.
•Turn the pork shoulder onto the other side and leave for another 5 hours.
•Shred the meat into pieces and serve hot.

Keto Slow Cooker Sweet Ham

INGREDIENTS:

1.5kg Ham
1.8oz apple cider vinegar
1 ½ tsp artificial sweetener
1 tsp water
1/2 tsp brown sugar
1 tbsp brown German Mustard

INSTRUCTIONS:

•Combine artificial sweetener (about 2 tbsp) with water and pour this into the bottom of the slow cooker.
•Mix the rest of the ingredients and rub over the meat parts of the ham ensuring not to season the fat part,
•Place the ham into the slow cooker and allow to cook for 7 – 8 hours.
•Remove the cooked ham from the slow cooker into a platter.
•Pour the juices and serve with salads or eggs.

Spicy Tomatoes Pork in Crockpot

INGREDIENTS:

2 tablespoons olive oil
2 pounds pork (shoulder or tenderloin) cut into 1-inch chunks
2 teaspoons garlic salt and pepper to taste
4 cloves garlic crushed
4 large jalapeno peppers fresh, seeded, diced
1 yellow pepper fresh, seeded, diced
1 red pepper fresh, seeded, diced
8 ounces mushroom quartered
2 teaspoons ground cumin
¼ cup onion sliced
2 tomatoes diced

INSTRUCTIONS:

•Pour the oil into a skillet and heat well.
•Rub the garlic salt and pepper on the pork and season well.
•Place the seasoned pork in the heated skillet and allow both sides to brown well.
•Transfer the browned meat to the crockpot.
•Use the same skillet and saute the mushrooms, peppers and garlic until soft and tender.
•Toss in the ingredients to the crockpot along with the cumin, tomato and onion.
•Cover and leave for about 4 hours or more until the meat is well cooked and tender.

Crock Pot Steak with Vegies

INGREDIENTS:

Smothered steak tenderloin with vegetables.
1 tsp garlic powder
1 cup pieces or slices mushrooms
2 large onions. Quartered
2 large green bell peppers, 3/4" strips
1 lb beef tenderloin
2 oz water
1/4 cup butter buds

INSTRUCTIONS:

•Use a non-fat cooking spray and spray the crockpot prior to using.
•Place the steak, mushrooms, quartered onions and peppers in the crockpot.
•Place the garlic powder, butter buds and water in a bowl and mix until the butter buds is completely dissolved.
•Pour the liquid over the vegetables and toss the ingredients.
•Place lid and cook for about 4-5 hours on High or 8-9 hours on low.
•Slice the beef into pieces and lay on a platter.
•Transfer the vegetables and the juice from the crockpot onto the platter.
•Serve with the steak.

Slow Cooker Foil Garlic Chicken

INGREDIENTS:

3 pounds bone-in chicken breasts or thighs—or whole chickens
1 tablespoon Better Than Bouillon Beef
1 tablespoon granulated garlic
2 tablespoons dried onion flakes
1 tablespoon freeze-dried parsley
Fresh ground black pepper
2 tablespoons gluten free tamari—or coconut aminos
Unfiltered extra virgin olive oil

INSTRUCTIONS:

•Place an aluminum foil in a baking pan
•Place the chicken breasts rib side facing up and smear each piece with the bouillon paste (about 1/3rd)
•Rub both sides of the meat with garlic, onion and pepper.
•Sprinkle the pieces with soy sauce, tamari, coconut aminos and olive oil.
•Cover with foil and place in the pan and cook in the oven for about 2 hours on 300F.
•Gently remove the foil and allow the chicken to cool for about 30 minutes.
•Shred the chicken and serve with pan juices.

Crock Pot Chicken Lettuce Wraps

INGREDIENTS:

24 oz boneless skinless chicken breast
1 celery stalk
1/2 onion, diced
1 clove garlic
16 oz fat free low sodium chicken broth
1/2 cup hot cayenne pepper sauce
for the wraps:
6 large lettuce leaves, Bibb or Iceberg
1 1/2 cups shredded carrots
2 large celery stalks, cut into 2 inch matchsticks

INSTRUCTIONS:

•Place chicken, celery, onion and garlic in your crockpot.
•Pour the broth over the chicken and if it does not cover the chicken add a bit of water.
•Cover with lid and cook for 4 hours on high.

Crispy Fried Chicken with Pork Rinds

INGREDIENTS:

1.5 pound Boneless chicken breasts sliced into strips
1 package Plain Pork rinds
1 egg
2 tablespoons heavy cream
2 tablespoons Frank's Red Hot Sauce
1 packet Powdered ranch dressing mix
Cooking oil
Salt and pepper to taste

INSTRUCTIONS:

•Rinse the chicken and dry using kitchen towels.
•Whisk the egg, ¼ of the ranch mix, cream and hot sauce together in a bowl.
•Dip the meat strips in the sauce for about 5-6 minutes.
•Pour the cooking oil until it comes to about 1" high and heat well.
• Place the Pork rinds in a sealable bag and crush them well and season with the balance ranch mix.
•Transfer the seasoned meat strips into the bag with the pork rind.
•Shake the bag for the ingredients to mix and season well.
•Move the chicken strips onto the heated oil and turn both sides.
•Allow the meat to cook and transfer them onto a platter.
•Remove the excess fat using paper towels.
•Leave for about 5-10 minutes to cool and serve.

Slow Cooker Rosemary and Sour Chicken

INGREDIENTS:

2 tsp. garlic, minced
2 tsp. paprika
2 tsp. rosemary
1 tsp. salt
1 tsp. pepper
4 tbsp. olive oil
2 lemons
1 chicken
1 cup chicken stock (or water)
potatoes & veggies

INSTRUCTIONS:

•Preheat the oven to 425F.
•Remove the peel of one lemon and insert in the cavity of the chicken.
•Combine the oil and the spices and season the meat with half of the mixture.
•Rub the balance quantity of the spices on potatoes and vegetables.
•Slice the lemon and place the slices along with the veggies on a pan.
•Pour the chicken stock over the ingredients.
•Spread the chicken on top of the other ingredients and bake for about 1 ¼ or 1 ½ hours until the meat is well baked.
•Serve with steamed veggies.

Chicken with Cheese and Scrambled Eggs

INGREDIENTS:

4 eggs
1/2 chicken breast, cooked and shredded
1/2 cup cheddar cheese, grated
2 strips chopped peppers
2 tbsp. onion, chopped

INSTRUCTIONS:

•Break the eggs into a bowl and whisk well for about 35 seconds.
•Mix in the shredded, chopped and grated ingredients.
•If required, add a little milk.
•Place all the ingredients on a skillet and leave on a low heat.
•Adjust seasonings by adding salt and pepper.
•Tastes delicious with yogurt or fruit.

Herb Lemon Chicken in Crockpot

INGREDIENTS:

2 chicken breasts
1 tsp. oregano or whatever herbs you like
1/2 tsp. salt
1/2 tsp. pepper
2 tbsp. butter
1/4 cup chicken broth
3 tbsp. lemon juice
2 garlic cloves, minced

INSTRUCTIONS:

•Mix the herbs, salt and pepper in a bowl.
•Rub the mixture on the chicken breasts.
•Heat the butter in a pan and brown the chicken pieces on both sides.
•Place the browned chicken in a slow cooker.
•Pour the broth and lemon juice into a bowl and add the garlic.
•Mix the broth well and pour over the chicken.
•Cook for about 5-6 hours on low.
•Can be served with veggies.

Spinach and Chicken Tortilla Pizza

INGREDIENTS:

1 tortilla
1/2 chicken breast
1 tsp. minced garlic
1 tbsp. pizza sauce
1 tbsp. sliced marinated artichokes
2 tsp. boursin cheese
1/4 cup of shredded cheddar cheese

INSTRUCTIONS:

•Preheat the oven to 450F.
•Heat olive oil in a pan and saute the chicken and the garlic until the chicken is cooked.
•Spread sauce over the tortilla and place them on a pizza pan.
•Add boursin cheese, artichokes and chicken and top up with shredded cheddar cheese.
•Leave in the oven for 12-15 minutes until the cheese melts and golden in color.

Slow Cooker Red Pepper Chicken

INGREDIENTS:

A standard slow cooker
2-3 pounds of boneless, skinless chicken breasts (frozen is fine)
1/2 cup Kraft Zesty Italian Dressing (substitutions for a lower carb Italian dressing should be fine, but I like this one)
1 packet of Hidden Valley Ranch dressing mix
3/4 TBSP Minced Garlic
1 TBSP Chili Powder
3/4 TBSP Cumin
1/4 tsp Cayenne Pepper
1/2 tsp Kosher Salt
A couple of shakes of Crushed Red Pepper
1/4 Cup Water

INSTRUCTIONS:

• Place the liquids and the spices in a bowl and mix well.
• Pour the mixture into the slow cooker just to cover the bottom.
• Toss in the breast pieces and add the balance mixture.
• Leave for about 8-10 hours on low or high on 4-6 hours.
• Remove the meat and if not already falling apart, shred using a fork.
• Place the meat once again in the slow cooker and leave for one hour.
• Remove and enjoy!

Slow Cooker Meatloaf Recipe

INGREDIENTS:

1 14 oz jar pizza sauce (divided)
1 beaten egg
1/4 cup chopped onion
1/2 cup chopped green pepper
1/3 cup dry bread crumbs
1/2 tsp Italian seasoning
1/2 tbsp minced garlic
1/3 cup shaved Parmesan
1/4 tsp black pepper
1 lb ground beef
1/2 lb hot pork sausage
1 cup shredded mozzarella
Diced fresh parsley for garnish (optional)

INSTRUCTIONS:

•Place three pieces of aluminum foil inside a slow cooker.
•Place 2/3 cup of the pizza sauce and the egg and mix well.
•Keep the balance ½ cup of pizza sauce aside.
•Toss in the onion, bread crumbs, green pepper, seasoning, garlic, black pepper, Parmesan, beef, sausage and mix well.
•Form the mixture into a shape of a loaf.
•Place the loaf on top of the aluminum foil.
•Cover with lid and cook on low for about 8-10 hours or high on 4-6 hours.
•Sprinkle the loaf with the balance pizza sauce and the shredded mozzarella.
•Place lid and cook for about 20 minutes until the cheese is well melted.
•Remove the loaf with the use of the foil pieces.
•Discard the foil pieces and serve.

Conclusion

Thank you again for downloading this book!

I hope this book was able to help you discover some amazing Keto Recipes. The next step is to get cooking!!!

Finally, if you enjoyed this book, then I'd like to ask you for a favor, would you be kind enough to leave a review for this book on Amazon? It'd be greatly appreciated!

Thank you and good luck!

Check Out My Other Favorite Keto Diet Books

Below you'll find some of my other favorite books that are popular on Amazon and Kindle as well. Simply click on the links below to check them out.

Ketogenic Diet: 365 Days of Keto, Low-Carb Recipes for Rapid Weight Loss

Ketogenic Recipes: 50 Low-Carb Breakfast Recipes for Health and Weight Loss

Salad in a Jar: 50 Mason Jar Salad Recipes to Grab and Go

Ketogenic Recipes: 50 Low-Carb Breakfast Recipes for Health and Weight Loss

Keto Recipes: 50 Low-Carb, Ketogenic Diet Lunch Recipes for Health and Weight Loss!

Ketogenic Diet Dinner Recipes: 125 Quick, Easy Low Carb, Keto Meals

If the links do not work, for whatever reason, you can simply search for these titles on the Amazon website to find them.

FREE Gift - Keto Holiday Recipes

As a "thank you" for purchasing this book, I want to give you a gift absolutely 100% Free

Click Here to Download Keto Holiday Recipes

Or go to http://freebookbonus.com/keto-recipes/

Printed in Great Britain
by Amazon